DECORATION ON FABRIC

DECORATION ON FABRIC

PAULINE BROWN

GUILD OF MASTER CRAFTSMAN PUBLICATIONS LTD

First published 2001 by
Guild of Master Craftsman Publications Ltd,
166 High Street, Lewes,
East Sussex BN7 1XU
Copyright © GMC Publications Ltd 2001

ISBN 1 86108 213 4

Editor: Nicola Wright
Book designer: Joyce Chester
Book photographer: Chris Skarbon
Cover designer: Ian Smith
Cover photographer: Christine Richardson
Illustrator: Penny Brown
Typeface: ITC Garamond and ITC Fenice
Colour separation: Viscan Graphics (Singapore)
Printed and bound by Kyodo Printing (Singapore)
under the supervision of MRM Graphics,
Winslow, Buckinghamshire, UK

10 9 8 7 6 5 4 3 2 1

ACKNOWLEDGEMENTS

MANY THANKS to all the embroiderers and textile artists who generously lent their work and photographic material, which has greatly enhanced the visual impact of the book. My thanks also go to the following manufacturers and suppliers who provided materials for experimentation:

Applicraft, Hampton, Middx; Colourcraft (Colour & Adhesives) Ltd, Sheffield; Design Warehouse Ltd, Hayling Island, Hants; Dylon International, London; Epson (UK) Ltd, Hemel Hempstead, Herts; Fashion 'n' Foil Magic, London; Lazertran Ltd, Aberaeron, Ceredigion; Levermore Workshop World, London; Make Your Mark, York; Noel Dyrenforth, London; Oliver Twists, Chester-le-Street, Co. Durham; Pentel (Stationery) Ltd, Swindon, Wiltshire; Rainbow Silks, Great Missenden, Bucks; Ribbon Designs, Edgware, Middlesex; Staedtler (UK) Ltd, Pontyclun, Mid Glamorgan.

Unless otherwise credited, all the work photographed in this book is by Pauline Brown.

CONTENTS

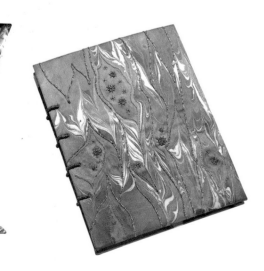

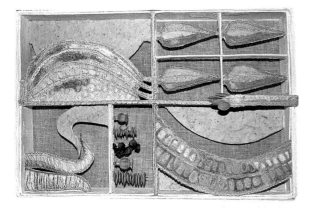

INTRODUCTION

ADDING DECORATION is one of the basic ways of giving individuality to fabric. Whether you are creating a simple embroidered edging or an elaborately painted effect, you can use your imagination to achieve interesting and exciting results on pictures, wall hangings, and all types of clothing and soft furnishings. You may also choose to continue the traditions of many centuries by adding embroidery or appliqué in the Western manner or try out those of the East by using the resist techniques of batik and tie-dye.

'MANUSCRIPTS AND MAGNOLIAS' MAGGIE PHILLIPS
18 x 25IN (46 x 64CM). *An idea taken from the 'Book of Kells' with painted background, burden stitch roundels and appliquéd flowers in painted and cut velvet*

Traditional Techniques

Embroidery has been a time-honoured way of embellishing fabric and today you have a choice of hand or machine stitching. Although hand embroidery is time consuming, its effect is quite different from that which can be achieved by machine, particularly the group of raised and three-dimensional stitches which adds texture. These can be used for all types of projects from panels and wall hangings to garments and items for your home. Machine embroidery has now developed in an imaginative way and the dissolvable fabrics have extended the range of effects you can create.

Appliqué can be worked either by hand or machine and has the advantage that it is a quick and easy method of adding large areas of texture and pattern to a project.

Clothing

One of the most obvious applications is to decorate clothing. Although fashions may come and go (tie-dye may be popular for one season, ribbon appliqué for the next) you can add a touch of up-to-the-minute originality to ready-made clothes or to those you design yourself. This can be anything from a simple cotton T-shirt with rubber-stamped or painted design to the most intricately beaded evening gown.

T-shirts are one of the easiest garments to decorate. They can be painted with all-purpose paints, pens or crayons, covered with stencilled designs and photocopied images or you can use one of the resist methods such as batik or tie-dye. If you are inexperienced you can start by experimenting on old T-shirts before you commit your ideas to brand new garments.

Evening wear is an obvious candidate for elaborate treatment – metallic paints and foils can be combined with appliqué in rich fabrics whilst embroidery can elevate a garment to designer status. You can scatter stitches or beading all over or concentrate the ornamentation at the collar, cuffs, seams or hem. Smart day dresses or separates could be decorated with leather or suede appliqué, wool embroidery in thick yarns or heavy braids stitched as an edging. Casual clothes allow plenty of scope for painting, printing, stencilling or dyeing.

Children's wear can be decorated with a whole range of techniques as long as you choose those which will stand up to hard wear and laundering. Brightly coloured laser–printed motifs can be transferred to T-shirts and tops, trainers can be painted with metallic or three-dimensional paints. Your children's efforts with transfer paints can be ironed on to clothes made of synthetic materials.

Garments for older children and teenagers can be decorated with quick and easy appliqué which can be machined to jeans or jackets. Traditional smocking may have gone out of fashion for babies and toddlers, but ribbon appliqué or embroidery can make a pretty effect on party dresses or christening robes.

'SUMMER GARDEN' (DETAIL) GRETA FITCHETT.
Appliquéd nasturtiums, with hand and machine embroidery

Contemporary Techniques

In recent years textile artists have been influenced greatly by the large number of exciting new products which have come on the market. To add sparkle and theatricality to your work there are lustrous metallic fabrics and threads; foils in gold, silver and copper, as well as hologram finishes, can all be applied to fabric. Fabric paints are available in pearlised and iridescent colours. These can be sponged, spattered or printed, and dyes can be applied using tie-dye, batik or simple dipping. Glitter and puff paints add a three-dimensional effect, and

transfer paints and crayons are another option.

The wide availability of photo and laser copiers and inkjet printers has introduced new ways of transferring images to fabric. You can either work from your own designs or adapt your personal photographs or those chosen from magazines. It is advisable to remember that if you are using someone else's work, the question of copyright may apply.

Combining Techniques and Experimenting

The main skill in combining techniques is to achieve a satisfactory balance between the various elements of the design. You should decide what is the most important aspect of the surface treatment. An elaborate batik fabric may need little further embellishment except perhaps the scattering of a few beads and stitches or the added texture of quilting.

However, many painting and printing methods can be very effectively used in the same project. There are several approaches you can adopt. You can add embroidery, beads or ribbons to a painted or dyed background; print some fabric and embellish it with metals and foils; photocopy an image and add an overlay of spraying or sponging.

If you are adopting this type of approach it is advisable to try out your ideas on a piece of scrap fabric or even paper. In this way new images and techniques will come to mind and you will be able to produce a totally original piece of work.

Whether you wish to work in a traditional or contemporary way, the materials and products which are available today will encourage you to use your imagination and create interesting and exciting work. The techniques in this book are just a starting point – they can be adapted and adjusted, combined or used alone. Experiment and, above all, have fun!

Detail of the back of a jacket by TERESA SEARLE.

PAINTING
AND
DRAWING

◆

ALL-PURPOSE PAINTS

PAINTING TECHNIQUES

FABRIC MARKERS

SILK PAINTING

ALTHOUGH in theory you can draw and paint on fabric with a number of ordinary paints, felt tips and crayons, in most cases a more satisfactory result can be achieved by using specialist products. These have the advantage that they are produced to give the greatest effect on particular types of fabric. Most do not stiffen the fabric, will retain their fastness and stand up to washing or dry-cleaning. Used alone they make interesting and beautiful patterns, pictures and designs. If areas of the design are covered or masked (see page 11) and the paint spattered, sprayed or sponged, the effects are limitless.

MARGARET GRIFFITHS 'WILLOWS'. *Fabric painted background embellished with hand stitches*

SILK TIES ROSIE DANIELS. *A selection of silk-painted ties using a variety of different techniques*

Fabric paints can also be incorporated in an embroidery or appliqué project. Clothing of every type lends itself to being embellished with this type of decoration. Children's and sportswear looks good with bold motifs whilst evening clothes may require a more subtle or luxurious treatment with iridescent or metallic effects. Soft furnishing items from table and bed linen to cushions, blinds and curtains also provide an opportunity for creative decoration.

There are three main types of fabric paint – all-purpose fabric paints, silk paints and transfer paints (see page 28). They can all be mixed to create an infinite range of shades, diluted or extended for paler tints and thinner consistency and applied in many different ways. In all cases, wash the fabric to be painted before use, particularly new fabric which usually contains a dressing that may adversely affect the stability of the paint.

ALL-PURPOSE PAINTS

These are available in a range of basic colours, plus iridescent, pearlized and metallic finishes. The colours are intermixable so you can start with a small selection of primary colours plus black and white. They are suitable for every type of fabric though smooth surface cottons, satins and synthetics are best for initial experiments. Interesting results can however be achieved with fluffy or ridged fabrics depending on the method of application. Most makes are made fast by pressing with a hot iron. You can apply them with a brush or sponge or try spraying, spattering or stencilling (see pages 15-17). If diluted with water or used on dampened fabric, you will find that they can also be used effectively as background colour washes. They are suitable, too, for a number of printing techniques (see page 28).

Purchased daffodil stencil with oil paint stick colouring

Basic preparation and technique

1 Prepare the painting table by covering it with a sheet of plastic. Protect surrounding areas.

2 Wash, dry and iron the fabric.

3 Tape the fabric to the work surface with masking tape, or mount it in an embroidery or batik frame.

4 Apply the paint using your chosen method .

5 Allow the paint to dry thoroughly or speed up the process by using a hair dryer. Iron the fabric from the reverse side to set the colour, making sure that the iron is first set to the correct temperature for the fabric.

Masks for Painting and Spraying

A mask is a piece of card, paper or an adhesive product which prevents paint or spray from infiltrating areas of a design where colour is not required. The design can be simple or complex and different types of mask can be used to create motifs or add texture and pattern. Masks can be used for all types of paint, which can be sprayed, spattered or applied with a stencil brush. You can also experiment with oil sticks, transfer paints and crayons.

Stencils

The most obvious masks are stencils which have the advantage that they can be re-used for repeat designs or different projects. Stencils can be made of heavy paper, card, special waxed stencil paper, acetate or sticky-backed plastic. Ready-made stencils with floral, classical or nursery motifs are available from DIY stores together with repeat patterns and friezes. Specialist patchwork shops sell quilting stencils which consist mainly of outlines of traditional designs such as hearts and flowers, and borders with feathers and chains. For painting and spraying choose a bold simple shape. You can also cut your own stencils using a craft knife and cutting board or a hot stencil cutter.

Cutting stencils

1 Draw the design on paper and divide it into sections. For example, separate the petals of a daisy from its centre, making sure that there are 'bridges' i.e. small divisions, between each section.

Drawing a design for adapting to a stencil

2 Trace the stencil design on to the chosen card, paper or acetate using bold firm lines. If you are using sticky-backed plastic draw the design in reverse on the backing paper.

3 Cut out the separate sections using a craft knife or scalpel and discard them or keep to use as a negative image stencil (see page 12).

Cutting out a stencil with a scalpel

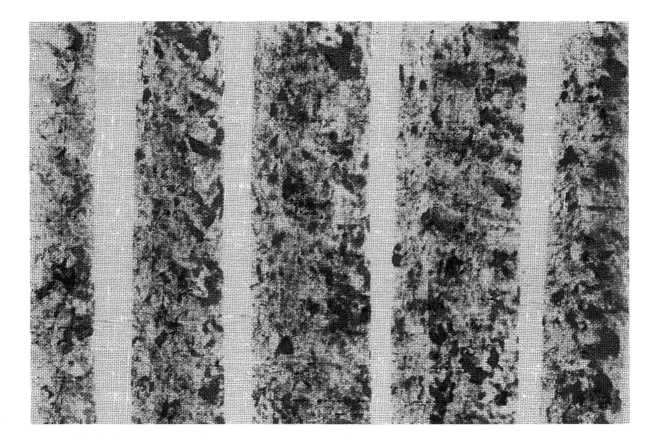

Using a hot stencil cutter

This tool is used with a special polyester film and heats to the required temperature. Place the polyester with the drawn design underneath on the special mat and draw the heated tool along the design lines to cut out the required shape.

Masking tape

This is available in several widths from stationers and DIY stores and in a low-tack variety which will not mark even the finest fabrics. The thicker type is more reliable for designs where any seepage would spoil the effect. It makes a good mask for geometric designs and borders and gives a crisp edge; the edges can be cut into wavy or zigzag shapes and holes can be introduced for added variety.

To cut the tape to shape stick a length to your cutting board and use a craft knife. Pull off the tape gently and replace it on your fabric which has been taped to a flat surface ready for painting or spraying. The same mask can be used several times if care is taken in lifting and replacing it.

Masking tape makes a formal mask for sponging

Other masks

Besides conventional sencils, you can create many exciting effects with other masks. Different types of mesh, such as metal meshes in square or diamond format (see page 124), sequin waste and needlepoint or rug canvas, make interesting patterns and textures. You may be able to discover other items around the home, such as sieves, cheese graters etc which can be used to make innovative masks. All of these can be used alone or, if you prefer, in conjunction with larger stencils. Simply place or tape them to the surface and paint or spray through the apertures. Wipe clean after use.

Interesting effects can also be created using leaves, flowers or twigs which are temporarily fastened to the surface with double-sided tape or a tiny rolled up piece of masking tape. These will produce a negative image which can either be used alone or alternatively emphasized with quilting or embroidery.

PAINTING TECHNIQUES

Using a brush

Shake the jar before use to mix the paint thoroughly. Transfer to a saucer or palette and mix the colours if necessary, without diluting with water. Always mix up sufficient paint for the entire project as it is difficult to reproduce exact shades. For fine details and small scale precise designs select a fine brush and paint in the normal way. Only add water if absolutely necessary, as too thin a solution will seep along the grain of the fabric and spoil the effect. Make sure that you allow one colour to dry before you embark on an adjacent area. Larger areas of solid colour can be painted with a slightly larger brush, but it is generally better to use a different method such as sponging or spraying.

You can also experiment by using a large brush at an angle or by stippling with it to create different marks on the fabric. For a watercolour effect, suitable for a background for further embellishment such as embroidery or beads, you can wet the fabric first and apply sweeps of colour with a large brush, blending the colours whilst the background is still wet.

Fabric paint brushed randomly using a large brush

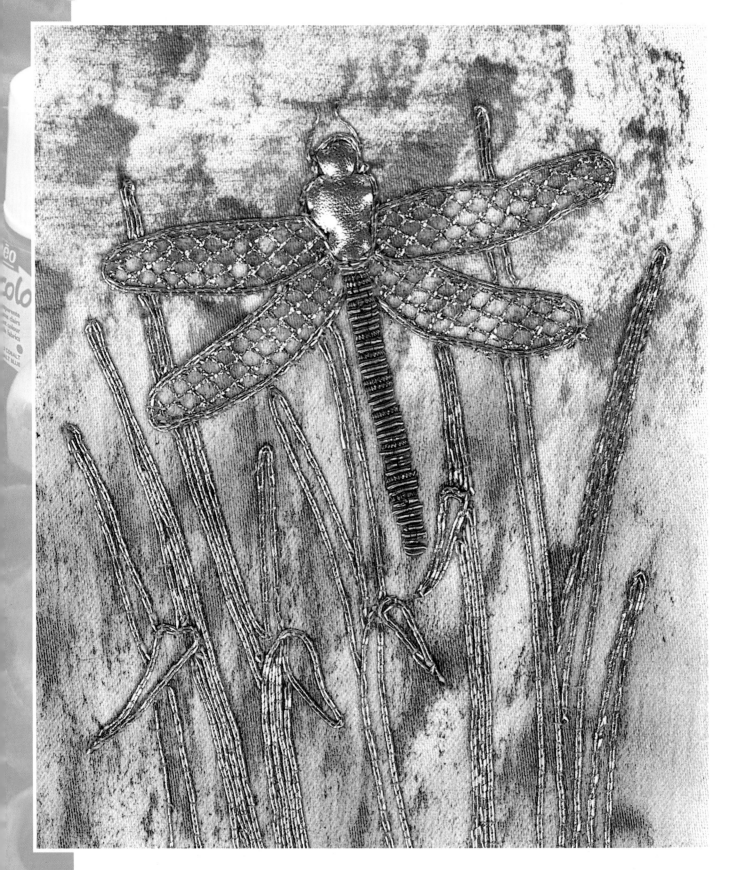

*Fabric paints sponged in different directions to create a
background for a metal thread embroidery*

Sponging

This is a simple method of applying paint with or without masking the fabric. Use a small piece of dry natural or synthetic sponge, dip it into the paint in your palette and lightly dab it on the surface of the fabric. You can overlap the sponging and use a variety of different colours, to make all-over background or textural patterns. It is sensible to try out different effects on a spare piece of paper or fabric before committing yourself to the actual project.

An alternative to sponge is to use a scrunched up piece of chamois leather or polythene bag for applying the paint. Pieces of synthetic sponge can be cut into precise shapes, such as squares, triangles or rectangles and used as printing blocks (see page 33).

Toothbrush spattering

This method can be used as a background in one or more colours and also looks effective with masks of all types. The result is less regular than spraying (see page 16). Protect around the outer areas of the fabric with paper and mask off any other areas as required. Dip an old toothbrush in the fabric paint, which you have poured directly from the jar undiluted. Use the paint sparingly to prevent drips. Holding the head of the brush away from you, take a piece of stiff card and draw it towards you across the bristles, directing the paint on to the fabric.

Everyday objects such as keys, coins and washers make interesting masks for toothbrush spattering

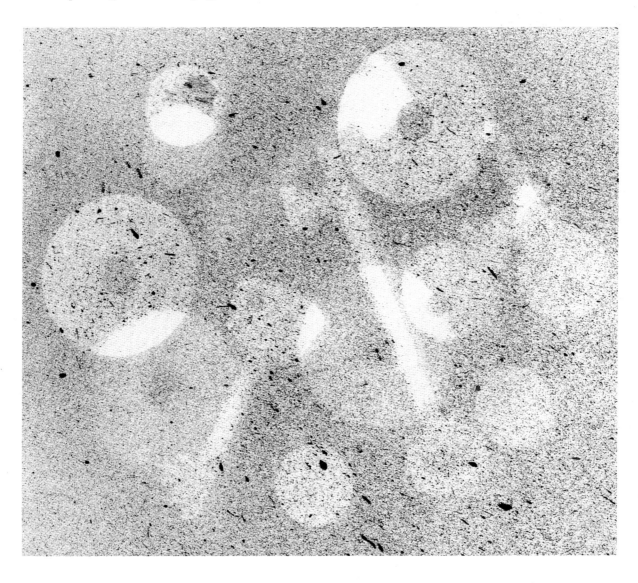

Spraying

Spray guns and airbrushes are available from graphic design stores and are either attached to a compressor or to an aerosol containing the propellant. Depending on the sophistication of the equipment, you can make various adjustments to regulate the flow of the paint which should be thinned with water to the consistency of single cream. Make sure there are no lumps, as these will block the flow of the paint.

Spraying through a stencil and mesh using a spray gun

1 Mask all parts of the design that you do not wish to be sprayed, and cover the surrounding areas with newspaper.

2 Hold the spray gun about 15–20cm (6–8in) away from the surface and using a rhythmic motion, move it steadily across the surface and back again. Do not spray too heavily in one spot, but apply a light coat.

3 Allow to dry and respray with the same colour for a denser effect or a contrasting shade in some areas of the design.

Stencilling

Stencils can be made from a variety of different materials (see page 11). Their designs have a unique quality in that each element of the motif is separated from its neighbour and when paint is applied through the cut-out spaces a fragmented stylized effect emerges. You can stencil by painting with a stencil brush, or with any of the sponging, spattering or spraying methods that are described above.

1 Prepare your work surface in the appropriate way for the painting method.

2 Position the stencil on top. If it is intricate or if you are spraying hold it in place with masking tape. Otherwise simply hold it with your non-working hand.

3 For painting use a stencil brush with undiluted fabric paint. Paint in the shapes, stabbing the brush down vertically. This can be done lightly for a stippled or mottled effect or more heavily with the paint forced down between the fibres to completely colour the fabric.

An effective stencil with an elaborate arrow design. Note that, as in all stencilling, each element of the motif is separated from its neighbour

Stencilling with a brush for a positive image

4 Wash and dry the brush thoroughly between applications of different colours.

5 Allow the paint to dry and remove the stencil. Heat fix the paint with an iron.

6 You can make a negative image by using the cut-out segments of the stencil as a mask and painting around them.

Using stencil segments to create a negative image

FABRIC MARKERS

Sketching and line drawing on fabric is an attractive alternative to painting larger areas of colour. You will find fabric markers particularly appropriate for their ease of use and for their immediate effect. You can draw designs directly on clothing, decorate accessories or incorporate them on panels and pictures. Details can be drawn and thick or thin lines used alone or added to painted, sprayed or printed designs. There is a large number of different markers available which are either permanent or can be made fast by ironing in a similar way to all-purpose fabric paints.

ELSPETH KEMP 'CITY ROOFTOP GARDEN' (DETAIL). *Fabric paints and markers are used as a basis for machine appliqué in organzas* (photographed by Ad Shots Studio, Hertford)

Fabric pens

These come in a wide range of colours and several widths, so are suitable for fine or heavy lines, and also with care can be used for colouring in larger areas. They can be applied in exactly the same way as felt-tip pens and work best on smooth light-coloured fabrics. Fluorescent and metallic colours are also available.

Fabric crayons

These are similar to wax crayons and available in a small range of colours which can be over-laid or blended with the fingers to produce greater variety. Their effect is greatest if used on light-coloured fabrics, though the lighter crayons will work satisfactorily on darker shades. They are suitable for natural fibres or those which do not contain a large percentage of synthetics, because they need to withstand ironing at a high temperature in order to make the colour permanent.

1 Work on a hard smooth surface and iron the fabric well.

2 Draw in the normal way or use the crayon with even strokes in one direction to create a regular solid effect.

3 To set the colour, cover the drawing with a sheet of plain paper and iron with as hot an iron as the fabric will allow.

These crayons are particularly effective for rubbings. Choose a textured surface – a carving on a piece of furniture, a rough floorboard or garden fence, or embossed or engraved metal – and tape the fabric to it with masking tape. Using the crayon on its side in order to cover a wide area, rub over the textured surface and fix the colour by ironing.

Oil paint sticks

These chunky card-covered crayons are made of a mixture of wax and oil paint and come in a wide range of colours, including metallics, fluorescents and iridescents. They can be blended

Fabric pens are sketched spontaneously on to cotton fabric

to create a huge range of different effects. They become permanent after about 48 hours after which they should be ironed to fix the colour. The protective skin has to be removed from the end of the crayon to reveal the colouring matter and this reseals itself within a few hours to prevent it drying out.

Oil paint sticks can be applied in many ways, with or without masks or stencils. They can be drawn on the fabric in the normal way and are also good for making rubbings (see above). For stencilling or areas of colour which need greater control, apply a coat of paint stick on the stencil or a piece of card. Pick up the colour using a stencil brush or toothbrush and transfer it to the appropriate area of the design.

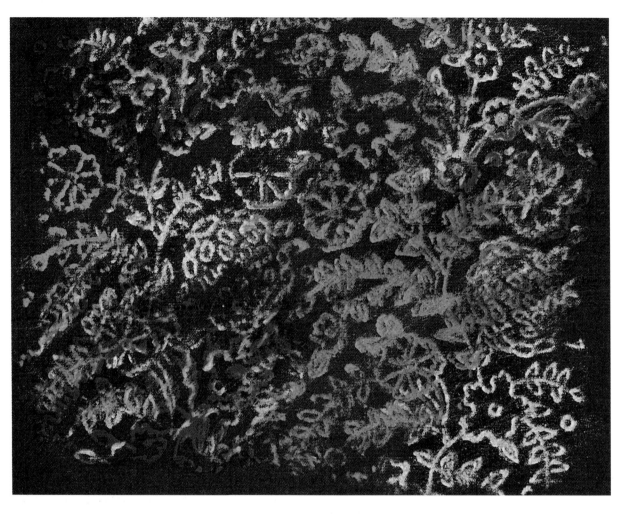

Oil paint sticks are effective for this rubbing of an Indian wooden printing block

Glitter and puff paint tubes

Three-dimensional fabric paints can be used to create pearlized, glossy, glitter and puff effects on most fabrics and come in a limited range of interesting colours. They are applied directly from their plastic bottles or tubes which have a nozzle attached and can be washed by hand after 72 hours. Simply hold the nozzle just above the surface of the fabric and squeeze gently so that the paint emerges. Leave to dry flat, preferably overnight. Puff paints expand with heat so the design should be bold and you should allow space between lines. Apply in the same way as the other three-dimensional paints, allow to dry thoroughly and press for about a minute from the reverse side with a hot iron to make them expand.

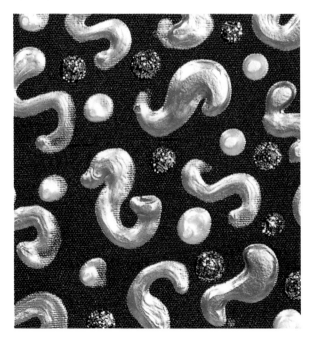

Dark coloured fabric makes a good contrast for glitter paints

SILK PAINTING

Silk painting has become extremely popular in recent years not only for scarves and clothing but also for panels. The paints, which give a lustrous transparent effect to the silk, are watery in consistency so that the liquid flows by capillary action along the fibres of the fabric. The colours can merge with each other or each element of the design can be separated by a barrier of gutta resist in order to outline the motifs or define the shapes.

There are two main types of silk paint. The original and professional range is available in a wide selection of lustrous colours which can be mixed together and flow easily. The colour is made fast by steaming, which can be done professionally or in a pressure cooker. The second type of silk paint, also available in a good range of colours which are intermixable, is not so liquid so that results are stiffer. However, they have the advantage of being made fast by ironing, so for beginners are a quicker and simpler option. Both are washable and dry-cleanable when fixed.

Although you can experiment with different types of silk, it is best to begin with a light-weight pongee which will allow the silk paints to flow satisfactorily. You can then move on to crepe satins, jacquards or chiffons. These are available from specialist suppliers who also stock a range of ready-hemmed scarves and ties, as well as fashion accessories and cushion covers.

The fabric should be framed up either in a rectangular frame or for small projects in a circular embroidery hoop. Special three- or four-pronged architect's pins are best.

Preparation and framing

1 Tape the design to your working surface with masking tape, ensuring that the silk is taped firmly and smoothly on top.

2 Lightly trace the design through using a dotted pencil line.

Tracing the design on to the silk

3 Pin the fabric to the frame making sure that the grain is straight. Start at the centre of the top edge and pin at 12mm (½in) intervals, working towards the sides.

4 Fasten the bottom edge in the same way, stretching the fabric taut.

5 Complete the two sides, pinning the centre points and work towards the ends, pinning one side and then the other.

Pinning the silk to the frame

Background washes

Having framed the fabric, use a large brush or sponge and apply the paint rapidly, because it tends to dry quickly. This can be done either on dry fabric or on that which has been previously lightly dampened. Several colours can be used which will blend together to produce secondary hues where they merge. If you allow the paint to dry between colours a line will be evident, though you may be able to use this effect to your advantage.

Salt and alcohol effects

A shimmering effect can be made by sprinkling salt on the wet or dampened painted fabric and shaking it off when dry. You can experiment with different types of salt from ordinary cooking salt to large grained sea salt. For the opposite effect, medicinal alcohol or surgical spirit, available from chemists, disperses the silk paint and can be applied with a cotton bud or a small brush. For both these methods it is best to use strong colours.

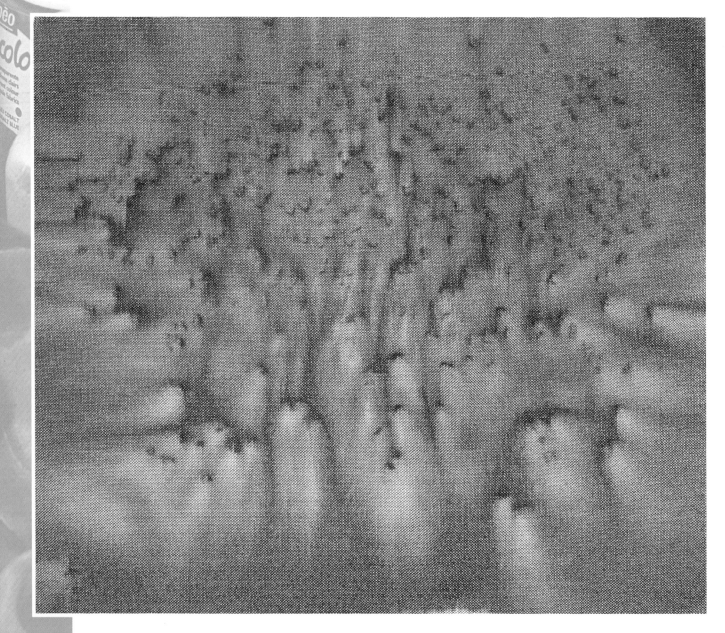

Salt effect on silk using large-grained sea salt

Gutta resist

Gutta is a liquid which is most often used as a resist of fine lines which prevent the silk paints from flowing to other areas of the design. There are two types of gutta, one rubber, the other water-based, which are available in jars, bottles or tubes in several colours including clear, black, gold and silver.

Some of these are equipped with a nozzle through which you can squeeze the gutta. Alternatively you can transfer the gutta to a small plastic pipette with a special plastic or metal nozzle for fine lines. Gutta can also be applied with a brush, sponge or stamp. As with wax resist (see page 55), it is important that the gutta penetrates through to the back of the fabric and when isolating shapes or motifs must totally enclose the image. The gutta can be thinned down according to the manufacturer's instructions to a consistency which allows it to flow satisfactorily, but is not so thin that it does not create a barrier.

Detail of a silk scarf with colour-washed background and flowers outline with gutta resist by DIANA WALKER

1 Mark the design and frame the fabric (see page 21).

2 Carefully draw the gutta dispenser along the lines of the design.

3 Allow the gutta to dry thoroughly before fixing, according to the instructions. You can speed up the process with a hair dryer.

Multicoloured silk square with colour-wash background overlaid with black by LIL DUBOWITZ

Overlaying effects

One of the most exciting ways of using silk paints is to overlay the fabric with different techniques. You may choose to begin with a delicate watercolour effect background wash, followed by a design of gutta resist made by outlining, stamping or sponging. You could then apply darker tones to some areas to make the resist visible. If you apply discharge paste (see page 51), further effects will be apparent. The above order could be altered or reversed for a different result.

Fixing colour by ironing

Depending on the type of silk paint you have used you will need to fix the colour to make it fast when washing. For iron-fixed paints, allow the paint to dry, then iron the fabric on both sides for two or three minutes with as hot an iron as the fabric will allow.

Fixing colour by steaming

Although fixing these paints is more complicated than the ironing type, the beautiful lustrous effects are worth the extra trouble. You may be able to find a supplier offering a steaming service or you can do it yourself using a pressure cooker. It is important that the painted silk does not come into contact with itself or with water during steaming.

1 Place the painted fabric between two pieces of calico or sheets of paper towel and roll it up carefully.

2 Roll the calico and silk in a sheet of aluminium foil, with the ends slightly crumpled to allow steam to penetrate.

3 Place either on the trivet or in the vegetable basket of the pressure cooker with about 2cm (¾in) of water.

4 Steam for around 45 minutes, following the manufacturer's instructions.

5 Allow to cool, then rinse the silk in cold water until clear.

6 Wash in warm soapy water. Finally rinse, dry and iron.

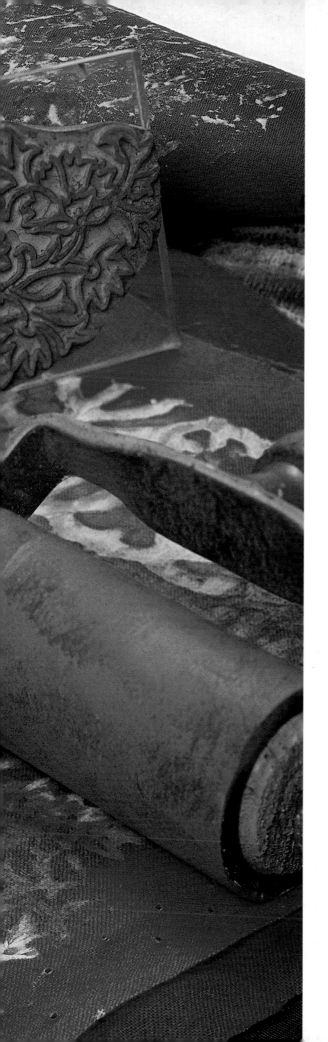

PRINTING

◆

TRANSFER PRINTING

BLOCK PRINTING AND STAMPING

THERE ARE many different ways of printing patterns and images on to fabric. These are nearly all easy to accomplish and need little specialist equipment, most of which is readily available or will already be in your possession. Transfer printing needs little practice and expertise as you can use trace or copy existing designs, while block prints can be versatile and used for many different purposes and on all types of fabric.

Transfer crayons are particularly effective for making rubbings

TRANSFER PRINTING

Transfer printing, as the name implies, involves transferring a painted or printed image on to fabric. Recent technology, including computers and laser printers, has increased the number of methods you can try, an advantage being that you can use ready-made designs. However, you should remember that some pictures may be subject to copyright and may not be used without prior permission. In most cases the transfers will appear on the fabric in reverse so you should consider this when painting or selecting an image.

Transfer paints and crayons

These are useful for trying out ideas, as the design is painted or drawn on to paper and then ironed off on to fabric. Many different painting techniques, such as sponging, spattering and stencilling can be combined to produce interesting effects. You can also use transfer paints for monoprints (see page 36), leaf prints (see page 34) or folded random prints to produce freestyle reflecting or symmetrical images. Errors can be cut away or covered with a clean scrap of paper or masking tape: smudges or small flecks of wax from transfer crayons can be removed similarly. If the design is a motif, cut it out and paste on to a clean sheet of paper.

The most effective use of transfer paints and crayons is restricted to fabric made of synthetic fibres, although reduced shades are possible when used on those with a mixture of man-made and natural fibres. It is advisable to make a chart of the available colours before you begin a project, because the shades painted on the paper inevitably differ from those which result when transferred.

Remember that the transferred design will appear in reverse, so particular attention should be taken when using lettering, numbers and asymmetric patterns. If you are decorating a garment such as a T-shirt, place a piece of card or several sheets of white paper inside so that the transfer does not go through to the back. Transfer painted projects can be hand washed in warm water. It is not advisable to use a tumble dryer.

1 Paint the design on to a smooth non-absorbent paper or use a cartridge paper for crayons. Allow the paint to dry for about 15 minutes. The crayons can be used immediately.

2 Cover the ironing table with several layers of newspaper with a sheet of white paper on top. Make sure that you set the iron to the correct temperature for the fabric.

3 Iron the fabric and place the transfer face down on top covered with another larger sheet of white paper.

4 Iron steadily and firmly over the design for several minutes, making sure it does not move. Lift one corner of the paper to check the colour, and continue ironing if necessary.

5 A second print can often be made, usually with reduced effect. For repeat motifs the original can be overpainted.

Folded prints

These can be made randomly or controlled to produce symmetrical motifs such as butterflies or landscape subjects such as mountains with reflecting lakes. The effect is enhanced if two or more colours are used.

Three separate folded prints cut out and transferred to form a butterfly design

1 Fold a sheet of paper in half and then open it out again.

2 Place drops of different coloured transfer paints on to one half of the paper fairly close to the fold and blend them with a brush to your satisfaction.

3 Fold the paper in half, pressing the paints so they spread out on to both halves of the paper.

4 Open up to reveal a symmetrical image. This can be used as it is or cut out to produce the shape you require.

Paper bag printing

This is a comparatively recent transfer method for colouring fabric using a by-product from the manufacture of printed fabric. This is a thin wrapping paper often used by florists or the cheap colourful paper bags favoured by market traders. The designs are ready-made so it is not necessary to be a competent artist to be able to produce interesting results. As with transfer paints and crayons it works on fabric such as

A geometric design made from a discarded paper bag

rayons, acetates and polyesters which contain synthetic fibres.

You will need to experiment with small scraps of paper and fabric to make sure you obtain a satisfactory print. Choose a brightly coloured design for best results. You can either use a whole sheet for transferring or cut out small motifs such as flowers and rearrange them to your liking on another piece of paper. Prints can be made on polyester fabrics such as ribbons, or used effectively as appliqué motifs.

1 Prepare the ironing board with several layers of newspaper and a sheet of white paper on top, and set the iron to the heat appropriate for the fabric.

2 Place the fabric right side up with the wrapping paper face down on top with a second sheet of plain paper on top of that. Iron firmly and evenly for at least two minutes, making sure the papers do not move.

Laser transfers

These are made by laser printing designs on to a special transfer paper, and the results can be applied to a large number of different surfaces from heavy fabrics and papers to metal and stone. There is a special silk transfer paper which gives a softer feel to the transfer and so is good for fine materials or projects which need to drape. These transfers should not be washed vigorously but they can be rinsed carefully in warm water.

1 On the shiny side of the transfer paper make a colour laser print on a photocopier.

2 Lay the transfer face down on the fabric and press with the iron on wool/cotton setting until they are stuck together.

3 Place in clean water, paper side down and leave until the backing paper can be peeled off. Lift the fabric from the water and wipe off any gum. Lay out to dry completely.

4 Cover with a sheet of baking parchment and iron firmly until the image is satisfactory. Allow to cool and peel off the parchment.

Photocopied transfers

If you are inexpereienced or nervous about producing original designs, transfer photocopying is an ideal method. The product for creating these is readily available and works with both colour and black and white photocopies which you copy in the usual way. Remember to check up on copyright, particularly if you are using the product for commercial purposes. For this method white paste is painted on the image before the print can be transferred to the fabric. It works best on light coloured fabrics. Articles with these prints should be hand washed in cool water. They should not be dry-cleaned nor should the actual transfer be ironed.

As with transfer paints and crayons the image is reversed so it is best to avoid subjects with lettering or numbers. Alternatively you can reverse the image automatically on some photocopiers or, failing that, photocopy it on to an acetate sheet, turn it over and then copy it again on to paper.

1 Photocopy your chosen image and cut to desired shape and size.

2 Wash and dry the fabric or garment to be decorated.

3 Tape the fabric to a work surface covered with a sheet of plastic.

4 Place the photocopy right side up on a sheet of waxed paper or foil and paint all over with a thick layer of paste so that the image cannot be seen clearly.

5 Position the photocopy face down on the right side of the fabric and press it down thoroughly, smoothing out any wrinkles.

6 Place a sheet of paper towel on top and using a roller, press vertically and horizontally for at least one minute until the edges are sealed and the image is secure. Allow to dry overnight.

7 Using a well-wetted sponge, soak the photocopy paper and gradually peel it off towards the centre of the image. Allow to dry.

8 Any remaining bits of paper can be removed with a damp sponge, though you may need to repeat this process several times until the image is clear. Allow to dry.

9 To seal the image rub in a few drops of the white paste, using a scrap of fabric and moistening the fabric thoroughly. Once again, allow the project to dry.

A computer-generated abstract design transferred to cotton fabric

Computer transfers

Special transfer paper suitable for inkjet printers is available from stationers which enables you to print clip art, scanned photographs or your own computer-generated designs to cotton fabric. If you want the image printed as the original you will need to select 'Flip Horizontal' on the printer. Print the design on to the transfer paper in your printer. Trim away any blank paper around it, leaving a 6mm (¼in) margin and iron the image off on to fabric or items such as cotton T-shirts or canvas bags.

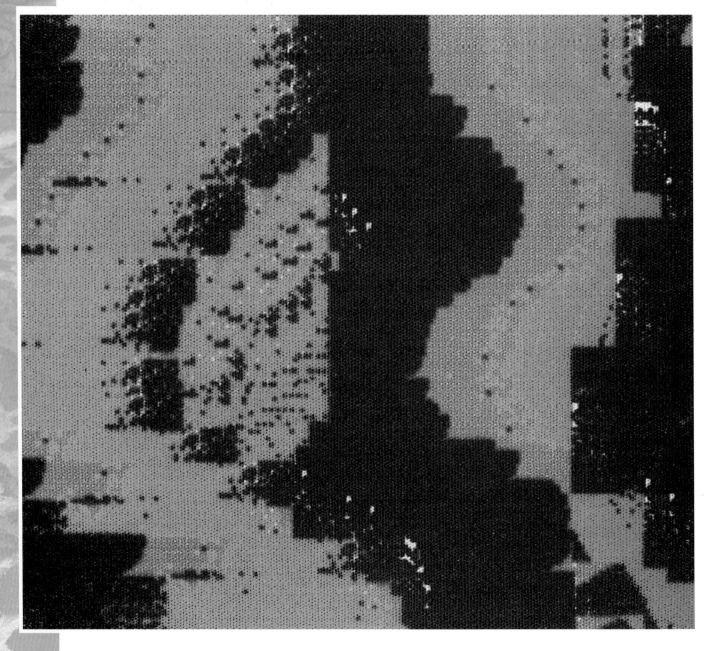

BLOCK PRINTING AND STAMPING

Block printing is one of the most ancient methods of transferring decorative motifs and patterns to fabric. It is particularly associated with the wonderful examples from India and other Far Eastern countries, where wooden blocks of teak or rosewood are still carved with intricate designs. In fact, blocks and stamps can be made from a variety of different materials from potatoes and string, to card and sponge.

The basic method of printing is simple and most fabric paints will work satisfactorily, provided they are not too thin. Some fabric paints can be used straight from the jar or can be made to the correct consistency with a thickener. Silk paints are generally not suitable as they are too runny. You can, however, print on paper with transfer paints before transferring the design to synthetic fabric.

Basic printing method

1 Prepare a smooth printing surface, with several layers of newspaper, a piece of old blanket or a double layer of felt.

2 Iron the fabric and tape it to the printing surface, keeping the grain lines straight.

3 Prepare a printing pad by folding a square of felt, blanket or similar padded fabric until there are several thicknesses.

4 Pour out a little fabric paint and spread it on the pad using a brush or piece of card.

5 Press the stamp or block firmly on to the pad and ensure that the raised surface is evenly covered with paint.

6 Press the stamp or block on to a practice piece of paper and lift off vertically. When you are satisfied with the result, recharge the block with the same amount of paint and print on your fabric.

7 Charge the stamp with paint for each application and wipe or clean the stamp thoroughly when changing colours.

For some types of block you may prefer to paint the surface using a paint brush or sponge instead of using a printing pad.

Vegetable prints

Potato printing is well known to school children as a way of making repeat patterns, and simple motifs. Other root vegetables such as carrots, swedes, parsnips and turnips make similar

Cut apple halves printed and embellished with stitchery and beading by ANNA GRIFFITHS

prints and can be cut to shape. A firm cabbage, cut in half or into segments, will give an interesting surface texture, whilst okra, cut across, produces a star shape useful for emulating tiny flowers.

1 Choose a close-grained potato and cut it in half with a sharp knife.

2 Cut into shapes or cut away the surface to form a raised pattern such as a star or simple flower. If you prefer you can place a paper template on the cut surface, draw round it and cut away the appropriate areas.

3 Wipe the surface dry before charging with paint and printing. You can either paint the surface or use a printing pad.

Leaf and flower prints

Experiments with different types of leaves and ferns will give interesting effects. Flowers with simple outlines such as hardy geraniums and daisies also produce satisfactory prints whilst

Hardy geranium leaves printed and used as a mask with pearlized fabric paints

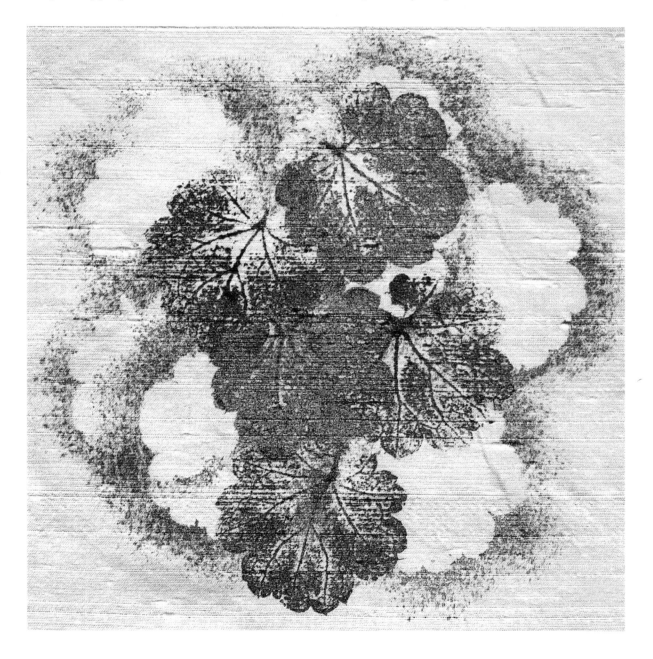

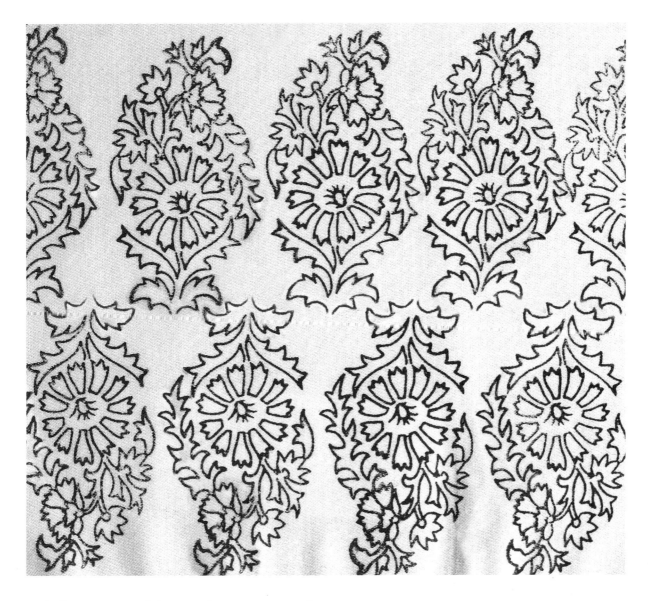

A rubber stamp design based on an Indian pine cone motif used for a repeat pattern

wide flat grasses and those with interesting seed heads make good accompaniments for printed flowers and leaves. Ears of wheat and barley are also effective.

1 Choose fairly soft leaves with prominent veins and paint them on the back.

2 Place the leaf paint side down on the fabric with a piece of paper on top.

3 Press with your fingers to print and carefully remove the paper and leaf.

4 Transfer crayons also work well on leaves. Place the crayoned leaf coloured side down on to synthetic fabric with a sheet of thin paper on top and press with a medium hot iron.

Rubber stamping

Rubber stamping has become very popular in recent years, for all types of paper crafts and you can purchase stamps in a wide range of designs. Some of these are also suitable for fabric printing, though it is best to choose bold clean designs rather than intricate subjects with delicate imagery. You can also make your own simple stamps using rubber or plastic erasers, cut to shape with a craft knife.

For best results use a printing pad and ordinary fabric paint, although you can paint

the surface of the stamp using a brush. Transfer paints (see page ooo) can be stamped on paper and ironed off on to synthetic fabric, or you can use foils for a metallic effect (see page ooo).

String prints

Printing blocks can be made of wood, MDF, or thick card such as foam board to which string is adhered. The designs can either be formal, realistic or geometric and you can experiment with different thicknesses and qualities of string or cord.

1 Draw the design on the wood or card block and cover with double-sided tape.

2 Peel off the backing paper and arrange cut lengths of string along the lines of the design, filling in the various areas as required. Secure the ends firmly.

A coil of thick garden string gives plenty of texture for a random string print

3 For a lasting finish, the block can be painted with a coat of acrylic varnish.

4 Print in the same way as for rubber stamps using a printing pad.

Lino prints

This is a traditional printing method for using on paper, but interesting effects can be produced on fabric. Squares of lino are available from art shops and you will also need a small selection of U- and V-shaped gouges to incise the design in the surface.

1 Transfer the design to the lino using carbon paper.

2 Using the gouges cut away the background and those areas which you do not wish to appear on the print. Always work with the tool directed away from you.

3 Charge the lino block by pressing onto a print pad or painting the surface with a brush and print in the usual way.

4 Place the lino face down on the fabric and press the image onto the fabric.

Miscellaneous blocks

It is easy to produce your own improvised printing blocks. Small realistic or abstract motifs can be cut from cork, thick card, foam board or corrugated card and glued to a wooden block. Thin household polythene sponges cut to shape are also a possibility, particularly for bold simple subjects. Layers of felt stuck together can be built up to form a printing block; thick lace or braids can be glued to a block and printed.

Monoprints

Monoprints have a unique quality due to the spontaneity and unpredictability of the technique, so the most suitable designs are freestyle, abstract or semi-abstract which will be enhanced by the texture of the print. Most fabric paints are suitable and if necessary can be made to the correct consistency with a fabric thickener. Acrylics are also possible though

these will stiffen the fabric. The paint is applied to a sheet of glass or plastic and printed off onto the fabric. Two or more colours will enhance the effect.

1 Tape the fabric to the printing surface.

2 Pour out the paint or paints onto the glass or plastic and spread firmly over the surface using a roller.

3 Draw the design or pattern in the paint using either your finger, a brush, a cocktail stick or a colour shaper.

4 Place the glass face down on the fabric and press hard all over or use a rolling pin.

The feathery tree-like forms of this monoprint are the spontaneous result of paint and fabric thickener applied between two glass plates and printed on to black fabric.

5 Lift the glass carefully to reveal the print which should be left to dry.

6 Different effects can be made by placing a second sheet of glass or plastic on the first painted sheet. Prise them apart and print as above.

7 If you prefer you can place the fabric on the paint-covered glass and allow the paint to seep into the fibres, or you can impress the design onto the back of the fabric.

DYEING

◆

DYEING METHODS

TIE-DYE

BATIK

MARBLING

DYEING METHODS

Dyeing fabrics, clothes and household linens can be great fun. You can revitalize tired and dull articles or simply alter the colour to fit in with your current needs. Home-dyed fabrics generally have a subtlety and luminosity which differs from the strong clear colours of commercial fabrics and you can combine or over-dye items to give innovative effects.

Manufacturers have made life easy with ranges of dyes for all sorts of fabrics. Large articles can be dyed in the washing machine, and smaller projects transformed in a bucket or saucepan. In every case follow the instructions carefully, checking the fabric content to ensure that the correct type of dye is used.

Make a note of the fabric's weight and the amount of dye used, so that you will be able to repeat the effect if necessary. In general, hot water dyes are suitable for natural fibres (including wool and silk), viscose rayon and nylon, while cold water dyes are best for cotton, linen and rayon, with lighter shades on wool, silk and polycotton.

If over-dyeing, remember that the base colour will combine with the dye. You will get an unsatisfactory result if you try to cover up stains. Threads can also be dyed to harmonize or to contrast with your hand-dyed fabrics, and ombré or shaded effects are also possible.

---

* Work in a well-ventilated room.
* Read the manufacturer's instructions carefully.
* Always wear rubber gloves and if using quantities of dye wear a mask or respirator.
* Cover your work surface and surrounding areas with plastic and newspaper.
* Clean up any spills immediately with kitchen paper.

Cold water dyeing

As with all types of dyeing you should wash, dry and iron fabrics before use in order to remove any dressing which may prevent the dye penetrating the surface. Dyes come in small tins or larger packets and can be inter-mixed. Specialist dyes are generally a little more complicated to use but produce vibrant colours. Most dyes require the addition of a fixer, such as salt or soda. Use within three hours.

1 Use a container large enough to accommodate the fabric easily and mix the dye carefully, taking note of the amount of water and dye.

2 Immerse the wetted article in the dye bath and stir gently for a few minutes.

3 Keep the fabric submerged for up to one hour and stir it at regular intervals until the density of colour is correct. Always remember that the colour will be much lighter when the article is rinsed and dried.

4 Remove from the dye bath and rinse thoroughly in cold water several times.

Hot water dyeing

There is a wide range of colours to choose from. Hot water dyeing is good for tie-dye as the shades are strong, and also suitable for discharging tie-dye as the dye is not colour-fast.

1 Follows steps 1 and 2 as for cold water dyeing (above) but, using a heat-resistant vessel, add the appropriate fixers.

2 Heat the dye to simmering and maintain for 20 minutes, stirring continuously to keep the fabric submerged.

3 Remove from the dye bath and rinse.

4 For wool and silk, bring the dye slowly to simmer. Stir very gently for 10 minutes. Rinse in warm water and do not subject the fabric to extremes of hot or cold water.

Machine dyeing

Machine dyes are especially formulated for automatic washing machines and are suitable for natural fibres such as cotton, linen, viscose and polycotton mixtures. The advantage of using a machine is that large items such as clothing or household linen can be evenly dyed. Simply follow the manufacturers' instructions carefully for a satisfactory result.

Ombré (or shaded) dyeing

Partially dyed fabrics or those shaded from dark to light or from one colour to another can look attractive for garments or household items. Although this method is rather time-consuming in order to achieve a smooth graduated effect, the results are worthwhile.

1 Choose a container large enough to accommodate the width of the fabric and use a dark coloured cold water dye.

2 Wet the fabric and, holding it with both hands, gently lower it into the dye. Immediately withdraw it very slowly, moving it to and fro. This action can be repeated until the desired effect is achieved. Do not allow the fabric to remain stationary.

3 Alternatively the fabric can be tacked and rolled on to a dowel which (see below) you rest on the edge of the container and gradually unroll into the dye.

4 Remove the fabric from the dye bath and hang to dry with the darkest area at the bottom.

Using a dowel to lower the fabric into the dye bath

Yellow and blue combine to make green for this ombré dyed sample

5 When dry, rinse and dry again.

6 To dye with a second colour, repeat the process at the other end of the fabric. Where the two dyes overlap a third colour will result.

Microwave tie-dyeing

This method requires the correct hand dye (see manufacturers' instructions) and is only suitable for small articles or samples in cotton, linen, silk and polycotton. Do not use for viscose rayon as it can emit fumes which are harmful. If you are dyeing a ready-made garment remove all metal attachments, such as zips, studs etc.

1 Dampen the fabric and then tie it up in your chosen way, binding it tightly.

2 Dissolve the dye in 250ml (½pt) of hot water, stirring thoroughly and then add another 250ml (½pt) water.

3 Immerse the tied bundle in the bowl and place it all in a plastic bag in the microwave set on 'high' for 4 minutes.

4 Remove the bowl from the oven, using a protective oven glove.

5 Rinse the fabric thoroughly in cold water and remove the bindings.

6 Rinse again and dry.

Dyeing threads

Threads which match your hand-dyed fabrics are a useful addition to your sewing materials. Wind the threads into a loose skein or into manageable lengths, and secure them so that they will not become tangled in the dye bath. Immerse them in the dye at the same time as the fabric. For a more random effect you can tie a number of knots in the hank or bind them tightly with yarn so that the dye only penetrates the outer strands. For a multi-coloured effect you can re-tie and over-dye with second or third colours. Threads of different fibres will take up the dye to varying extents, so you can produce a wide range of tones.

A selection of tie-dyed threads

Dyeing threads

TIE-DYE

Tie-dyeing is a resist process whose origins go back many thousands of years. Today it remains part of the rich culture of decorating fabric in Asia, while in the West it periodically becomes fashionable for clothing and accessories. Textile artists and embroiderers find its spontaneity attractive, as the range of effects is seemingly limitless and it can be combined with stitchery, beadwork and quilting.

The basic technique is to fold and tie the fabric in a variety of ways in order to achieve different patterns. The usual method is to tie up the fabric with string, but you can also use other types of yarn or rubber bands, bulldog clips and clothes pegs. The bundle is then plunged into either hot or cold water dye and those areas most tightly bound will resist the penetration of colour. It is advisable to choose a strong colour for maximum effect. Whilst a certain amount of chance determines the finished result, with practice you can reproduce similar effects.

After the first dyeing, the sample can be untied, refolded and tied in a different way, before dyeing with a second colour. The second dye will blend with the first to give four areas of colour, i.e. the background, the first and second colours, plus a combination of the first and second.

A selection of tie-dyed fabrics

Tying and folding

The way you tie and fold the fabric will determine the tie-dyed pattern. There are many folding techniques, but you should remember that the fabric on the inside of the sample will be least likely to accept the dye, so you must take care to arrange the folding in such a way that the darkest areas are where you wish them to be. The thickness of the string or yarn will also be apparent.

Marbled patterns

The random patterns of this simple technique are suitable for all sorts of items, particularly as background areas for embroidery projects since the effect can evoke skies, vegetation or watery scenes which can be further embellished with stitches. Over-dyeing with a second colour can be effective if the bundle is undone and re-tied.

1 Crumple the fabric in your hand, so that the proposed darker areas are outermost.

2 Tie up the bundle with string, cord, raffia or rubber bands, with the bindings criss-crossing the surface.

3 Alternatively, place the crumpled bundle in a plastic mesh bag and secure tightly with string or rubber bands.

4 Dye, rinse and carefully untie the bindings.

5 Rinse again and dry in the normal way.

Tie up a bundle of fabric to create a marbled pattern

Two-coloured marbled pattern

Sunburst designs using buttons at the centres

Circular and sunburst patterns

These are the classic tie-dye motifs and very easy to achieve. You can make a series of circular shapes by tying up objects such as buttons and pebbles. Bind each one tightly with string or rubber bands. For precise placement, you will find it easier to mark their positions with a pencil before you begin as the fabric becomes distorted as the tying proceeds. To make a sunburst design, tie a large stone or button in the centre of the fabric and bind the rest of the fabric at intervals to create concentric circles.

Bind tightly with string or rubber bands to create circular or sunburst designs

'STONES AT THE FOREST EDGE' ALISON KING (DETAIL).
Inspired by the stones at Kenmore, a mixed media triptych with handmade papers, batik, tie-dye, and paint

Rectangular patterns

Formal geometric patterns are suitable for all sorts of household items such as table and bed linen, as well as clothing. The fabric can be folded in half or quarters, or may be formed into accordion pleats, either on the straight grain of the fabric or diagonally.

1 Fold a square or rectangle of fabric in half and half again for a quartered design. Tie or clamp with pegs or bulldog clips.

Folding in half and half again and clamping

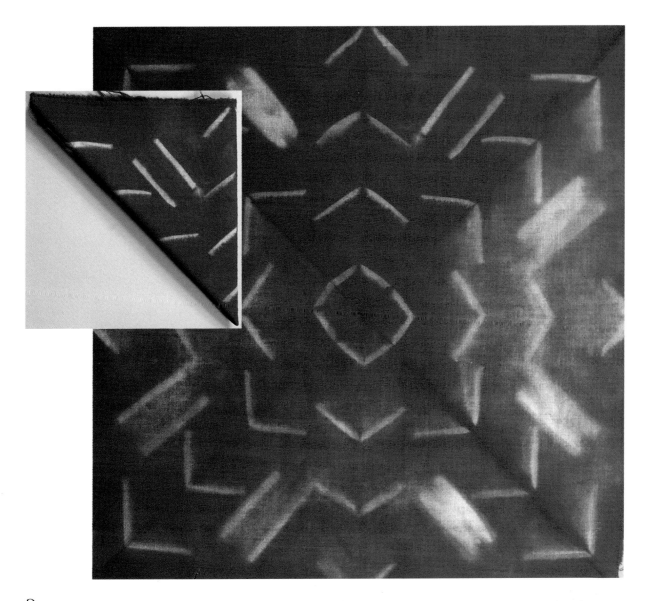

2 Fold a square of fabric diagonally in quarters to form a triangle and then in half again in order to produce a smaller triangle (see below). Clamp or tie as desired.

A square of fabric folded into a triangle and clamped with bulldog clips before dyeing

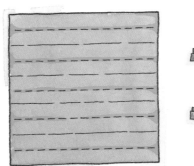

Folding diagonally in quarters and then in half again

Accordion pleats are suitable for striped designs and can be clamped or tied

Chevrons

Zigzag chevron designs are particularly attractive. The accordian pleats and folds should be precisely done with the central area on the outside.

1 Fold a rectangle of fabric in three lengthways, bringing the sides to the middle, and fold in half again, so that the centre of the fabric is outermost.

Linen fabric accordian pleated for a chevron design

2 Accordian pleat diagonally and tie up with the binding going straight across the bundle.

Folding and tying chevrons

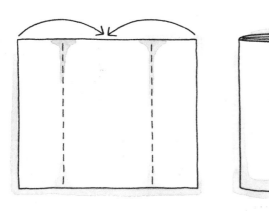

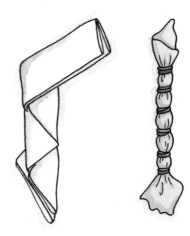

Mottled effect

This works best with a fine fabric such as lawn or silk, so makes beautiful scarves, lingerie or blouses. The effect can be suitable for different types of embroidery background, particularly garden scenes, and it can even emulate a snake-skin design.

1 Roll the fabric over a piece of thick cord.

2 Fold the roll in half and, holding the two ends of the cord together, push up the fabric towards the centre until you have a small bundle.

3 Tie the ends of the cord together and dye in the usual way.

Silk fabric rolled over a cord for a mottled effect

4 If a length of fabric, such as a scarf, is folded in half and the rolling started at the fold, the ends of the piece will be darkest.

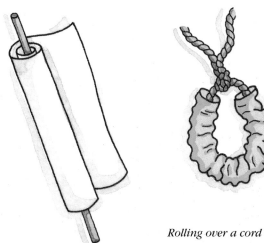

Rolling over a cord and securing

Tritik

This is an interesting development of tie-dye with the resist achieved by stitching with a needle and strong thread instead of binding or clamping. The results can be more defined than the usual tie-dye patterns. The fabric can be pleated, tucked, oversewn or gathered and the thread is then pulled very tightly. Fine fabrics which gather or manipulate well such as muslin, lawn or silk work best for this method.

To gather, make a series of running stitches in rows for an all-over pattern or two adjacent rows as the outline of a design. Pull up the threads and fasten securely. For a symmetrical design, fold the fabric in half and stitch through both layers. A zigzag machined line will give a good resist through several layers of fabric and

Stitching a scalloped border on folded fabric together with a spiral design

A variety of tritik borders including double scallops and tiny spirals

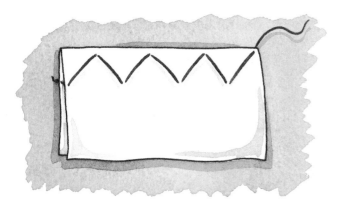

Stitching on a fold

need not be gathered. You can also make tucks in the fabric and work the gathering stitches through both layers. This will result in alternate strips of dark and light when dyed.

Discharge dyeing

Tie-dye patterns can be produced in reverse by a method known as discharge dyeing. Use fabric which you have previously hand-dyed in hot water dye or fabric paints which have not been fixed. You can also experiment with commercially dyed fabrics to see if the dye is stable. Proprietary brands of colour remover can be used or you can try a weak solution of bleach and water. In each case you should use the product with care and make sure that you read the manufacturer's instructions carefully.

Discharge paste is a specially prepared product which works well with both fabric paints and dyes and is particularly good for brushing on to the fabric or printing with a block or rubber stamp.

Detail of an embroidered velvet scarf with discharged areas by ANNA GRIFFITHS

BATIK

Batik is one of the most beautiful and intricate textile techniques. It can be used effectively in its own right for wall hangings, soft furnishings and clothing or can be combined with quilting and embroidery.

Like tie-dye, batik is a resist method of dyeing, but in this case the resist is made with wax applied to areas of the fabric to prevent the dye penetrating. This is done either with a brush, a small tool called a tjanting or a stamp known as a tjap. Nowadays, even in countries of the Far East where the craft has long been part of the national heritage, the method is often simplified by using fabric paints and wax in a similar way to silk painting with gutta resist (see page 23).

A silk batik piece based on travel to Morocco with hand and machine-stitched details by ROZ ARNO

Buddha design with spattered background

Another way of simulating batik is to paint a special liquid on the fabric, which when heat set, can be dyed in the normal way with cold water dyes. This method is particularly suitable for use by children, who should not be allowed to work with hot wax.

However, the traditional technique is to make several applications of wax, alternated with different coloured dyes, to build up the design gradually. One of batik's most distinctive characteristics is so-called 'crackle' – the irregular network of fine lines created by wax infiltrating tiny cracks.

The method is only suitable for silk, cotton and linen as synthetics will not stand up to the heat of the wax. Only cold water dyes may be used as hot water dyes would melt the wax.

Equipment and materials

Some specialist equipment for batik is necessary, including a thermostatically-controlled electric hot plate – it is not advisable to heat wax over the naked flame of a gas cooker. You will also need a wax pot for heating the wax. You can use a heavy double saucepan with water in the bottom and wax in the top. If you use an ordinary saucepan, you must take extreme care that the wax does not get too hot.

Place a heat-resistant mat close to the hot plate so that you can remove the wax pot from the heat as soon as the wax begins to smoke.

The fabric is pinned to a frame ready for waxing. Batik frames are made up of four pieces of wood which can be adjusted to accommodate different sizes of fabric, or you can use an artist's stretcher or an old picture frame in soft wood. For very small designs an embroidery hoop would suffice.

Tjantings are available from specialist craft shops, and are the traditional tool for making fine lines and dots. They have wooden handles and brass or copper reservoirs to hold the wax with a fine spout, or sometimes two spouts, through which the wax flows. Tjaps (metal stamps) can be home-made or purchased. You will also need a selection of cheap brushes of various sizes. These can be cut to shape for making double or treble lines. You can obtain ready prepared batik wax or make up a mixture of one-third beeswax to two-thirds paraffin wax. An alternative is microcrystalline wax.

Traditional batik sequence

The basic principle of traditional batik is that the design and its colours are built up with each application of wax and its subsequent dyeing.

Waxing white areas and dyeing yellow

Waxing yellow areas and dyeing red

1 Sketch the main lines of the design lightly on the fabric.

2 Mount the fabric in the frame (see page 21).

3 Wax those areas of the design you wish to remain white.

4 Dye in the first dye bath, choosing the lightest colour, for example yellow. Allow the fabric to dry.

5 Wax those areas you wish to remain yellow.

6 Dye in the second dye bath using the next darkest colour, for example red. This will combine with the unwaxed yellow areas to produce orange. Allow to dry.

7 Wax those areas you wish to remain orange.

8 Dye in the third dye bath, using the darkest colour, for example dark blue. This will combine with the unwaxed orange areas to produce brown. Allow to dry.

Waxing

The use of wax, particularly with a tjanting, requires practice. It can also be a dangerous pursuit, which means that extreme care should be taken. Never allow the wax to be left on the

Waxing orange areas and dyeing blue

heat unattended, and should it start to give off thick smoke, immediately remove it from the heat source. It is advisable to have a fireproof blanket and/or a fire extinguisher available in case of accidents.

1 Heat the wax in a double saucepan or wax pot, making sure that it is not more than half full. The wax will begin to smoke slightly at which time turn down the thermostat to control the heat.

2 Allow the brush or tjanting to heat up for a few seconds in the wax. Shake off the excess wax from the brush and do not fill the tjanting too full. Have ready a small pad of newspaper covered with a rag, for use as a drip-pad when you are transferring the brush or tjanting from the wax pot to the fabric.

3 Test the temperature of the wax on a spare piece of fabric. You will need to work quickly so that the wax does not cool down. It should be transparent and penetrate through to the back of the fabric. When using a tjanting, the wax should flow evenly through the spout. To test that the wax has penetrated thoroughly, hold the frame up to the light. Large brushed areas can be re-waxed on the reverse side if necessary, but it is important to get the tjanting lines correct as they cannot be redone.

Crackle

To produce the fine network of lines, which is one of the main characteristics of batik, you will need to use a greater proportion of paraffin wax to beeswax. If no crackle is required use more beeswax and a dye bath large enough to accommodate the fabric without creasing.

1 Brush large areas of fabric with wax.

2 Place the waxed fabric in the freezer or refrigerator for about 10 minutes so that it becomes brittle.

3 Crumple the wax in your hand. You can regulate this so that only those areas you wish to 'crackle' are creased.

*Hosta design showing tjanting lines for leaves with
brushed background*

Tjaps or stamps

In the Far East these printing blocks are made of an intricate latticework of metal sheets and rods, which are dipped in hot wax and stamped onto the fabric. You can make your own out of pastry cutters, or you can hammer some tacks or drawing pins on a block. When using tjaps, cover the work surface with waxed paper and tape the fabric in place ready for stamping.

Removing the wax

When the waxing and dyeing process is complete, you will need to remove as much wax as possible. This can be done by a combination of ironing and dry-cleaning.

1 Cover the ironing board with several layers of newspaper and a layer of kitchen paper. Place the batik on top with more kitchen paper and newspaper on top of this.

2 Set the iron to the appropriate setting for the fabric and iron off the wax through the paper, changing the papers frequently until the wax has been removed.

3 To soften the fabric and remove any residue of wax, you can take it to be professionally dry-cleaned.

A circular design using tjaps with waxed and crackled central area

Cold wax method

This product, available in a small bottle, is useful for quick projects or for use by children as it eliminates the danger of hot wax. It is suitable for use on cotton, linen and viscose, but not on 100% synthetics, silk and wool. You can also use it as a resist for stencilling, sponging and block printing.

1 Sketch the design lines lightly on the fabric. Mount in a frame or tape to your work surface.

2 Shake the bottle thoroughly and paint the design with the cold wax directly on to the fabric.

3 Allow to dry overnight or use a hair dryer to speed up the process.

4 Cover the painted area with a cotton cloth and iron for two minutes with the iron set to a cotton setting.

5 Immerse the dry fabric in cold water dye for 30 minutes in a dye bath large enough to accommodate the fabric without creasing.

6 Rinse and dry in the usual way.

7 Repeat the process to build up the design with additional colours.

Painted batik

If you prefer not to go through the various repeated stages of waxing and dyeing to build up a design, you can trace a single application of hot wax using a tjanting or fine brush along the outlines of the design in a similar way to gutta resist for silk painting (see page 23). Make sure that elements of the design are completely isolated by the waxed lines or the colours will run from one section to another. Paint different coloured dyes or paints between the outlines. The wax is then removed in the usual way. This method makes an attractive alternative to conventional batik, although it's fair to say that the traditional characteristics of the craft are not so evident.

BATIK CUSHION (DETAIL) ROZ ARNO

MARBLING

Marbling is a technique which has been used for centuries by bookbinders for making decorative covers and endpapers for books. To create marbled fabrics in the traditional way is extremely skilful, but you can now purchase marbling kits which offer a simple method of reproducing the characteristic swirling and feathered designs. These products work well on most fabrics, in particular satin or silk, which give a lustrous effect and are made fast by ironing. The limited range of colours can be pre-mixed before use to extend the range.

Apart from the marbling paints and gel you will need a flat plastic dish, such as a cat-litter or photographic tray, some cocktail sticks and a home-made comb fashioned from a lath of wood with nails tacked along one edge.

A selection of marbled fabrics

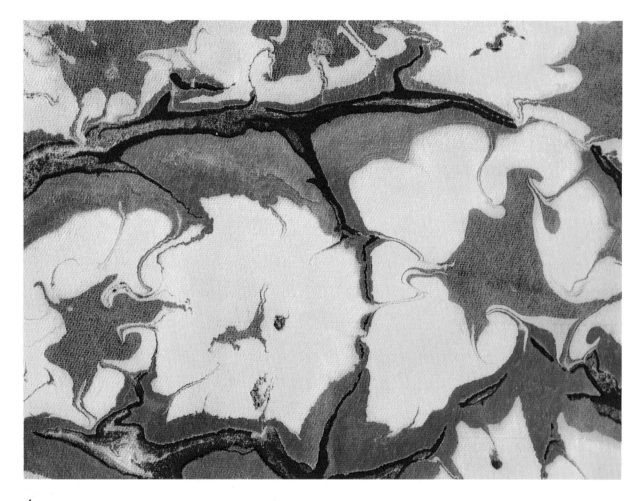

Multicoloured circular pattern

1 Following the manufacturer's instructions prepare the gel by dissolving the thickening powder in water, making sure there are no lumps.

2 Pour about 1cm (¼in) into the plastic tray and leave for one hour.

3 Using the dropper from the bottle of marbling colour, place drops of colour on to the surface of the gel.

4 Move the colours about to create the desired marbled pattern.

5 Lay a rectangle of fabric, smaller than the plastic tray, on to the marbled surface and leave it for a few seconds.

6 Remove from the gel and rinse under running water to remove excess gel and colour.

7 Lay flat to dry and heat fix with the iron set to the appropriate heat for the fabric.

Circular patterns

1 Place drops of a light colour alongside one another on the gel surface and allow them to spread.

2 Superimpose drops of different colours on to the first group, resulting in concentric circles.

3 If desired, use a cocktail stick to drag the colours into flower or other shapes.

Feathered patterns

Proceed as for circular patterns with concentric circles of different colours. Gently draw the marbling comb across the surface from top to bottom, continue if necessary until the desired effect is achieved, but do not over-work the design or it will become muddy.

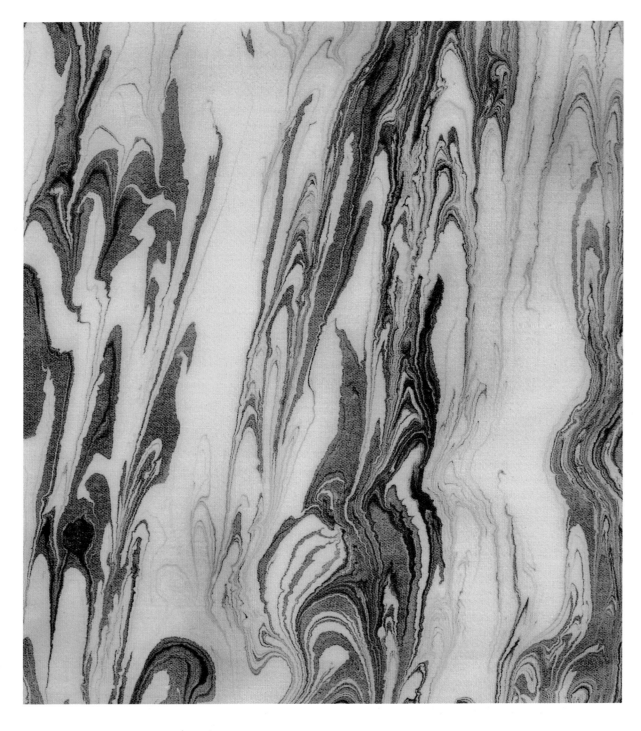

Green and black marbling on yellow cotton fabric

EMBROIDERY

◆

HAND EMBROIDERY

MACHINE EMBROIDERY

APPLIQUÉ

BEADS, SEQUINS, JEWELS
AND FOUND OBJECTS

RIBBONS, BRAIDS AND CORDS

HAND EMBROIDERY

Hand stitches are probably the most obvious surface decoration of fabric and have been practised for hundreds of years. The number and variety of stitches is infinite and the range of different threads available makes embroidery one of the most intricate and exciting and versatile forms of embellishment.

Simple embroidery stitches, such as chain, stem, buttonhole and satin stitch are generally in the repertoire of most needlewomen and basic instructions are readily available. In order to extend the effects of these stitches, it is worthwhile practising some of them to modify, adapt and alter their visual possibilities. Although traditionally stitches were worked in a very regular form you can adjust their scale and direction, work them haphazardly or use varying thicknesses and types of yarn.

Buttonhole stitch and chain stitch are two types which are particularly versatile. They can be worked with the individual stitches close together, far apart, long and short, slanted or crossing each other. Try these variations with other stitches, superimposing one row upon another or simply scattering them randomly over the surface of the fabric.

Although there are fabrics and threads manufactured specially for embroidery, you can work decorative stitches on a wide range of fabrics and use threads such as knitting and crochet yarns. Ready-made clothes and household articles can all be embellished although you may need to take into account the practicalities of washing or cleaning. If this is a consideration choose threads which have the same or similar fibre content as the fabric, otherwise you can create interesting surfaces and patterns with any type of yarn from raffia and twine to chunky wool or finest silk.

ANNA CHRISTY 'CORTINHAS I' (DETAIL). *Layers of silks, organza, muslin and hand-made silk papers with hand- and machine-stitched details*

Raised and three-dimensional stitches

To give an extra dimension to your work, there is a range of stitches which add pattern and texture in an exciting and interesting way. Some are brought into relief by means of base stitches which are then worked upon with an additional thread. One of their advantages is that the base stitch, which is often completely covered, can be worked in a thin thread which is easily stitched, whilst the top thread can be one which

'ABBEY FRAGMENTS' – *a mixed media piece based on elements from St Albans Abbey, Hertfordshire, England, with potato printing. Hand embroidery includes raised stem band on the columns*

does not go so readily through the fabric, thus creating heavy texture on a fine fabric. For these it is easier to use a twisted, non-stranded thread and to use the eye of the needle to weave through the surface stitches.

Some, such as spider's webs, woven wheels, raised herringbone, woven picots, raised cup, buttonhole loops and raised leaf are isolated motifs which can be used alone, massed together in groups to create textures or stitched in regular formation. Raised stem and raised chain bands produce a more solid effect which can be used as a filling stitch. Knotted stitches give plenty of texture, particularly when worked in chunky yarns. They include bullion knots and loops, together with the familiar French knot, and have many applications from the centre of flowers to thickly encrusted surfaces.

All these stitches should be worked with the background fabric mounted in an embroidery frame or hoop.

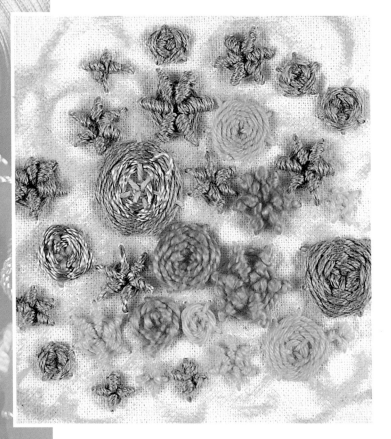

Woven wheels and spiders' webs

Woven wheels

These circular motifs are very versatile as, although the foundation stitches are usually completely covered with the weaving worked close together, you may leave the straight stitches showing at the perimeter, or change the colour and type of thread to create a pattern of concentric circles.

1 Work a foundation circle of an uneven number (usually five or seven) straight stitches radiating from the centre.

2 Continue with the same thread or thread up another long one on to a tapestry needle. Bring the needle out close to the centre of the circle.

3 Take the needle alternately over and under the straight stitches, working round the circle in a clockwise direction. You may find it easier to weave using the eye of the needle going over and under the radiating spokes first, particularly if the base threads are in a thick yarn such as wool, which could be split by the needle's point.

Spider's webs

This stitch has a similarity to the woven wheel, but you are not restricted to an uneven number of base stitches. The effect is such that the radiating stitches are raised with a flat surface between them. You can vary the effect by changing the colour halfway through, or leave the ends of the radiating stitches uncovered.

1 Work a circle of any number of straight radiating stitches as for woven wheels.

2 Bring the needle up close to the centre of the circle. Working on the surface as for woven wheels, take the needle forward under two stitches, back over the second stitch, then under it and the next one in a similar way to working back stitch.

3 Continue in this way around the circle, gradually loosening the tension until the circle is complete.

Woven picots

Picots were traditionally worked as a delicate edging on household linen or underwear. Nowadays, however, they are more often used with thicker threads to form three-dimensional flower petals or leaves. The dimensions can be altered slightly by using a long darning needle instead of a pin in order to create an elongated shape.

1 Insert a pin in the fabric to take up as much fabric as the size of the finished picot. Bring the needle out a short distance to the left of the pin, take the thread round the pin and insert the needle the same distance to the right of the pin.

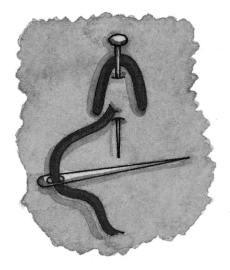

2 Bring the needle out alongside the left of the pin. Take the thread round the top of the pin as before. Begin weaving on this group of three threads, taking the needle under, over and under on the first run from right to left; then weave from the left to right going over, under and over.

3 Continue until the threads are completely covered. Gradually loosen the tension so that you maintain the triangular shape. Remove the pin and the picot will hang freely.

Woven picots and raised cup stitch

Raised cup stitch

Raised cup, as the name indicates, produces a small circular motif, useful as a single element, for example as a tiny flower-head, or when massed together, as a textural device.

1 Work a base of three small straight stitches in a triangle formation in a fairly thick thread such as pearl cotton.

2 Bring the needle out at one corner and work a series of twisted buttonhole stitches in a clockwise direction to cover the straight stitch foundation producing a raised circle.

3 To achieve the circular shape, make this stitch very small.

Raised fishbone stitch

This stitch is made up of a series of cross stitches, worked adjacent to one another over a base stitch.

1 Make a vertical stitch and work a cross stitch diagonally across it.

Raised herringbone, raised fishbone and raised leaf stitch

2 Work a second cross stitch just below and crossing the first. Repeat with several more similar stitches until the required fish or leaf shape is achieved.

2 Bring the needle out on the left just above the start of the first cross-over stitch and repeat the stitch several times gradually moving towards the vertical straight stitch to create the leaf shape.

Raised herringbone stitch

This variation on traditional herringbone stitch makes attractive leaf shapes which are also quick to do.

1 Work a small vertical straight stitch. Bring the needle up about 12mm (½in) below and take it through the straight stitch, but not through the fabric, from right to left. Insert it slightly to the right of where it emerged to make a cross-over stitch.

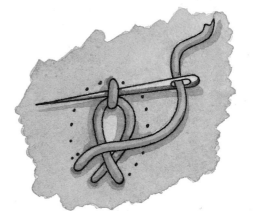

Raised leaf stitch

To get the best effect with this stitch use tapestry or double knitting wool to create the chunky raised leaf shapes.

1 Cut a narrow strip of card about 6 x 50mm (¼ x 2in).

2 Start at the top of the leaf and, using a thick thread such as pearl cotton or tapestry wool, bring the needle up alongside the strip of card. Work six or eight straight stitches alongside one another over the card, keeping it in an upright position.

3 Bring the needle up to the left of the previously worked stitches and thread it through to the beginning. Remove the card and pull the loops back to the left. Make a small straight stitch to form the stem of the raised leaf shape.

Raised chain band

The conventional way of working this stitch is to work a narrow ladder of base stitches with the overlaid stitches creating a braid-like effect. You can strengthen its impact by varying the width and length of the stitches and also of the distance between them.

1 Using a series of evenly spaced horizontal straight stitches, make a foundation of the finished shape.

2 Bring the needle up just above the centre of the first horizontal stitch. Take it down over and up under the first stitch to the left, but not through the fabric.

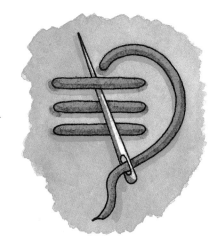

3 Bring the needle downwards under the first stitch to the right of the working thread and up through the loop. Repeat, keeping an even tension.

4 Work additional rows either side of the first to fill the shape.

5 The effect can be varied by working alternate rows in different directions – top to bottom and then bottom to top.

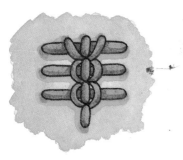

Raised stem band
This has a smoother effect than raised chain band, but in a similar way you can vary the distances between the base stitches, leave areas unworked or change the colour and type of yarn as you wish.

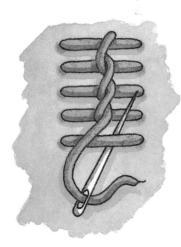

Raised chain and raised stem band

1 Work a foundation ladder of horizontal stitches as for raised chain band.

2 Bring the needle out above the first horizontal stitch. Then bring the needle down over and up under the first stitch. Repeat over the rest of the horizontal stitches as for conventional stem stitch but not through the fabric.

3 Work additional rows alongside

4 The effect of this stitch can be varied by bringing the needle out to left or right on alternate rows.

French knots

These tiny knots are used as flower-oftencentres, but they can be very versatile. They can be massed together for a thickly encrusted surface or combined with other three-dimensional stitches.

1 Bring the needle to the surface and hold the thread taut between the forefinger and thumb of your non-working hand.

2 Twist the needle twice round the thread and insert it halfway, just adjacent to the point from which it emerged.

3 Pull the twist down the needle so that it lies on the fabric, then push the needle through to the back of the work.

Bullion knots and loops

Bullions are an elongated form of knot and work best in a twisted thread or thick yarn, as stranded threads tend to separate and give an untidy result.

1 Bring the needle to the surface and insert it the required length of the stitch, bringing it halfway out again at the same place from which it originally emerged.

2 Wind the thread round the needle about six times. Then, holding the twist with your thumb,

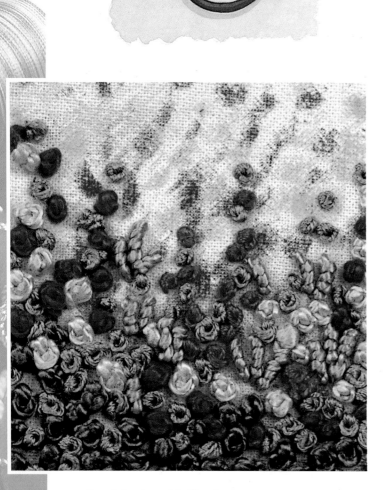

French knots and bullion knots

pull the needle and thread through the twist and out of the fabric. Pull the needle and twist to the right and insert the needle so that the twist lies smoothly on the surface.

3 To make a bullion loop, insert the needle and bring it out a very short distance away from the starting point and wind the thread round the needle many times. Continue and finish as for ordinary bullion knots.

Buttonhole bars and loops

Buttonhole bars are often used by dressmakers for fastening devices with a hook, but they are an attractive raised embroidery stitch in their own right. Worked in a radiating star formation, they make pretty flower heads.

1 Work two or three straight stitches one on top of the other to make a bar.

2 Work a series of buttonhole stitches over these, but not through the fabric. Bring the needle out at the left-hand end and, keeping

Buttonhole bars and loops

the working thread below the needle, take it under the straight stitches from top to bottom, bringing it through the loop. Repeat until the straight stitches are covered.

3 To make buttonhole loops, take up a tiny amount of fabric for the straight stitches but leave the threads hanging in loops. Work buttonhole stitch over the loops in the same way as for buttonhole bars.

ANN DANIELSEN 'BLUE LANDSCAPE' (DETAIL). *Overlaid fabrics are enhanced with various threads and beads to produce a heavily textured foreground*

MACHINE EMBROIDERY

Embroidery on the sewing machine is one of the classic contemporary ways of decorating fabric. Not only can it be relatively quick to accomplish but it also gives an entirely different effect from hand stitching. There are many machines on the market nowadays, including computerized versions, to aid the worker in producing motifs, borders and patterns of all types. However, in the same way as the ability to work with paint and a brush does not necessarily make the user a creative artist, so the ownership of a modern sewing machine does not mean you can produce exciting and original work. In order to do this, you need to study the manual to learn all the conventional methods, then practise effects and techniques before embarking on a piece of work.

Modern sewing machines are usually based on a zigzag function and, in addition to straight stitching and satin stitch, provide a large number of automatic stitches which can be used for formal patterns and borders. Different presser feet are also available which enable you to extend your repertoire of effects, to make raised, couched and looped stitches as well as double and triple rows simultaneously. For free-style machining the foot can be removed altogether so that the work can be moved around below the needle, creating a spontaneous and contemporary approach. With all machine embroidery it is advisable to try out the stitch, thread and tension on a spare piece of fabric as the work is tedious if not impossible to unpick.

Fabrics

Most fabrics are suitable for machine embroidery, although fine fabrics together with jersey and stretchy nylons are more difficult to handle and will benefit from being mounted on an additional backing fabric or an interfacing made specially for the purpose. For free machining or

'TURKISH CARPET' (DETAIL) GRETA FITCHETT. *Appliqué panel in a variety of different fabrics, embellished with free-machine embroidery*

work which is to be heavily stitched, it is advisable to back the work with a firm calico or cotton for your initial experiments. If you are machining on extremely fine fabrics there are products for backing the work which can be torn or washed away after stitching.

Threads

There is a vast range of threads produced specially for machine embroidery, which include shaded and metallics, cottons, rayons and polyesters. An interesting effect can be achieved by using two contrasting threads at the same time. Insert a heavy needle and thread up the machine in the usual way making sure the threads do not twist and go either side of the tension disc. Thicker yarns and cords, such as those which are made for knitting, crochet and embroidery, can be couched using the braiding foot or even wound on to the bobbin to create interesting textural effects.

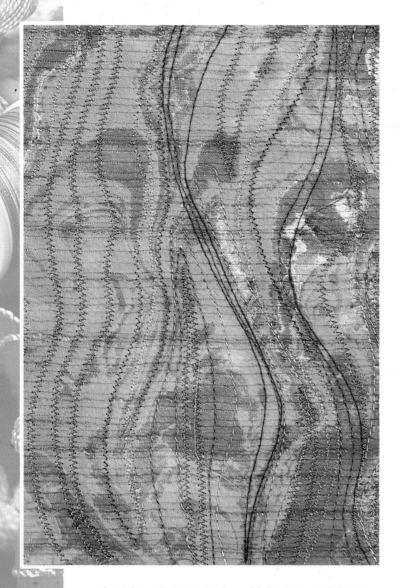

Straight and zigzag stitches add emphasis and direction to the marbled fabric

Needles

Machine needles come in sizes from very fine (70) to heavy (120). Choose one which suits the thread and fabric. You can also purchase twin and triple needles for multiple parallel lines, together with hem stitch and double hem stitch needles.

Tension

For normal stitching and using automatic stitches as they were intended by the manufacturer of the machine the top and bottom threads should be equally tensioned, so that they are linked precisely to produce a regular and even stitch. Some of the creative free-machining techniques require either the top or the bottom tension to be adjusted. This will depend not only on the type of stitch being worked but also the thickness of the thread either on top or in the bobbin. The top tension can usually be altered by means of the dial at the front of the machine; to tighten or loosen the bottom tension carefully turn the screw on the bobbin case. Experiment using contrasting colours for the top and bottom threads so you can easily see the results of making different adjustments until you have achieved the effect you require. If you attach some types of presser foot, the tension will also need to be altered accordingly.

Designs

Although single lines of straight stitching can produce a delicate effect, this may result in a rather weak design. A more effective way of approaching machine embroidery is to build up the stitching with closely worked or overlapping and massed rows so that a solid texture fills motifs or covers areas of the background surface. Experienced embroiderers are often able to stitch freehand without the design marked on the fabric. However, you may find it a help to draw a few lightly marked guidelines to give you confidence. If the design is more

Facing page: ALISON KING 'STONES AT THE FOREST EDGE' (DETAIL). *Mixed media with handmade papers, batik, tie-dye machine embroidery and acrylic paint*

precise, the main outlines can be drawn on tracing or greaseproof paper. This is then tacked to the top of the fabric and machine stitching worked along the marked lines through the paper which is later torn away.

Conventional stitches

The basis of machining is the use of straight stitching with the machine threaded in the usual way and using the standard presser foot. You can experiment with different types of thread, altering the stitch length and width. With the stitch width at its narrowest, work stitches in evenly or irregularly spaced rows, then overlap them or mass them closely together.

Zigzag and satin stitches are also worked with the presser foot attached. You can adjust the stitch width dial so that different widths of stitch are achieved and this is used in conjunction with the stitch length mechanism. To create a wide satin stitch, use the widest stitch width with the shortest stitch length. You can experiment with various adjustments and even alter the width as you stitch for an undulating or tapering effect.

Automatic stitches

Most modern machines include a variety of decorative embroidery stitches. These range from simple scallops, zigzags and border designs to lettering, flowers and other tiny motifs. Set the stitch width to its widest together with a short stitch length. Experiment with different widths and lengths to produce either solid or more open patterns. Using a variety of different threads, work the stitches either in formal rows or in irregular lines which overlap or cross, so that a texture is produced.

You can extend the range of effects by using different types of presser feet. Some come as standard accessories, whilst others can be bought as and when the need arises. With these, the fabric is automatically held in place and fed under the needle, and the effects are therefore limited to straight or wavy lines, unless the presser foot is lifted and the work turned. Some are used in conjunction with special needles.

Rows of automatic stitches in variegated threads make an attractive border

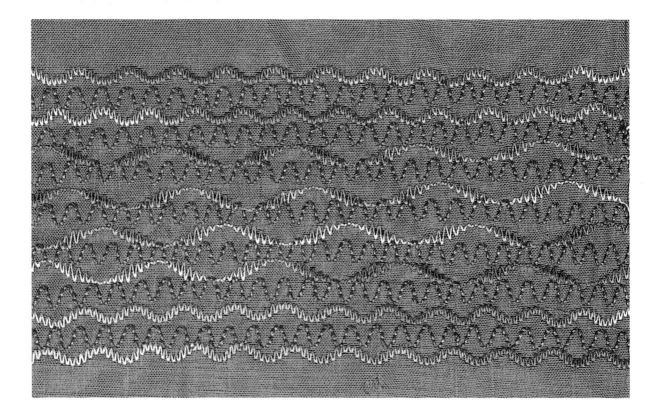

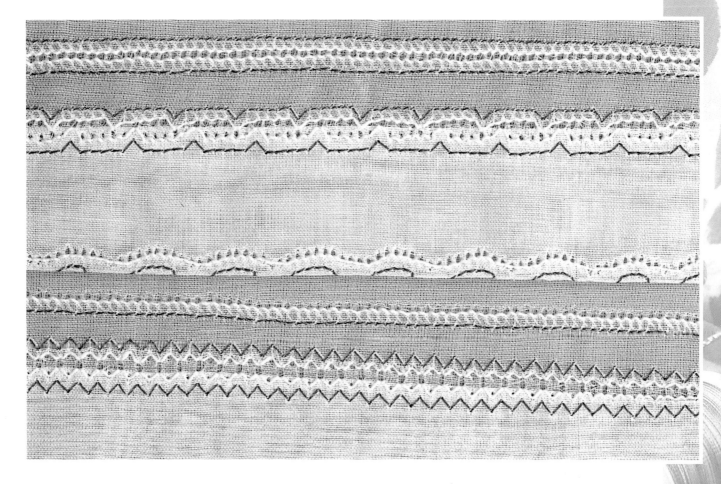

Twin and triple needles

For decorative designs which need parallel lines, such as border on sheets, pillowcases and table cloths, as well as garment hems and cuffs, these needles (available in different widths) are a way of ensuring regular spacing. They can be used in conjunction with a pin-tucking foot to produce raised lines with a thick thread under the fabric. Different coloured cottons can be threaded in each needle in order to add variety to the work.

Insert the needle in the normal way and thread up the machine with two adjacent threads; make sure that they do not twist and pass them either side of the tension disc. Proceed with the stitching in the normal way. If you are using a triple needle, wind the third thread on a bobbin and place it beneath one of the other reels on the left-hand reel pin. Thread up the three threads with those for the outside needles on the left of the tension disc and the middle thread on the right.

A delicate effect is achieved with hem stitching and automatic stitches

Hem stitching needles

Hem stitching gives a pretty effect on fine crisp fabrics such as organdie, organza or cotton lawn and can either be used in the traditional way for lingerie, babywear and linen, or you can create delicate effects for embroidered panels and pictures.

The single arrow-headed needle produces a series of regular holes in the fabric. Set the stitch width fairly wide and the length to short and proceed with a zigzag stitch. To make a second row, leave the needle in the work, before turning and sewing a second row with the needle piercing the holes on one side of the first row.

To use the double needle the machine is threaded with two adjacent threads. Make sure they are not twisted and are passed either side of the tension disc. Set up the machine for

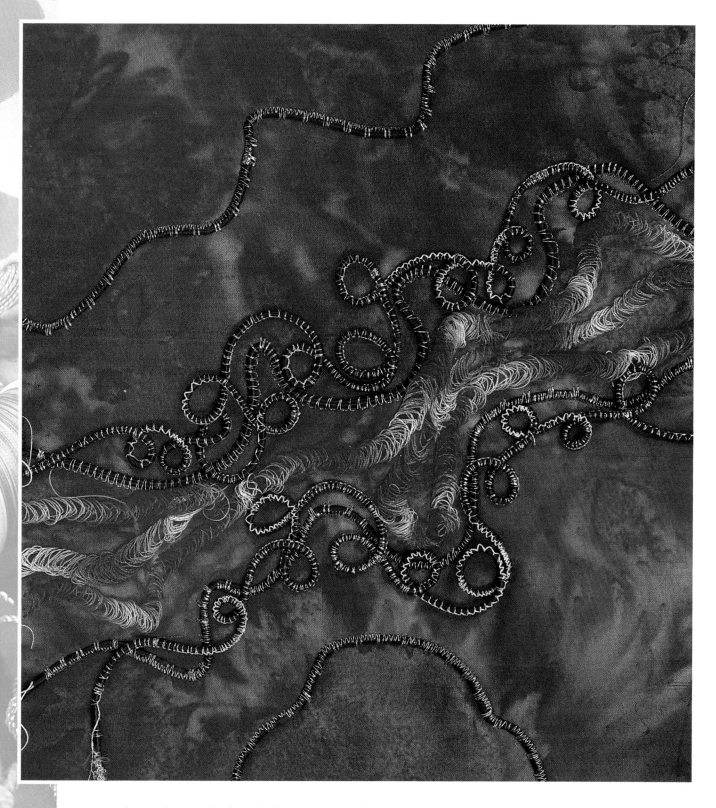

straight stitching and after the first row, turn the work and put the arrow-head needle in the first hole of the previous row. Zigzag and some automatic embroidery stitches can also be worked with these needles.

Cords attached with automatic stitches in metallic threads together with raised loops made using the tailor-tacking foot produce a highly textured piece

Presser feet

Most sewing machines are provided with a selection of standard presser feet, such as embroidery and zigzag, while others can be purchased as optional extras. The pin-tucking foot is used with twin and triple needles, and a transparent appliqué foot is useful as the edge of the applied fabric is visible. The tailor-tacking foot produces a textured looped effect and the braiding foot is indispensable for attaching narrow ribbons, cords and thick yarns, as well as for making wrapped cords.

Tailor-tacking foot

Although this foot was designed for making tailor tacks for dressmaking projects, if the stitch width is adjusted to wide and the length to short, a line of loops is produced. These will gradually slip off the foot, leaving a raised pile which is effective if the rows are worked close together. For solid areas of stitchery you need to lift the foot and regularly turn the work. Shaded and metallic threads are particularly effective.

Braiding foot

This type of foot has a hole in the foot-plate through which the cord or braid is threaded prior to stitching. There are several sizes, from the ordinary embroidery foot with a small hole for fine threads, to a larger version which can cope with narrow ribbons and thicker cords. Use a normal zigzag stitch or experiment with some of the automatic embroidery stitches.

Thread up the machine in the usual way with the cord threaded through the hole and under the foot. Set the stitch width to the width of the cord and the length you wish. Insert the background fabric under the foot and as you stitch the cord is automatically fed through the hole and couched in place.

Wrapping cords

Attach the braiding foot and thread up the machine as above omitting the background fabric. As you stitch, ease the cord through from under the foot so that it is wrapped by the machine threads.

Free Machining

One of the most popular ways of decorating fabric in a creative way is to work free machining, a method which is often likened to drawing with needle and thread. Besides allowing makers to express their artistic talents in a painterly fashion, free machining can be worked on dissolvable fabrics which when washed away will result in machine-made lace and free-standing items – motifs, jewellery and miniature boxes or bowls.

You can either use a darning foot or remove the presser foot altogether. In each case the feed dogs are lowered so that the fabric is not fed automatically beneath the needle. This enables you to move the fabric around by hand in any direction. Both methods have their advantages and a little practice will help you decide which you prefer. If you are working without a presser foot the fabric must be mounted in an embroidery hoop. This method is good for projects which are small enough to be contained within the perimeter of the frame, and you can see exactly where the needle is piercing the fabric. Using the darning foot enables larger scale work to be attempted without the need to continually move the frame from one area of the work to another.

Preparation and framing

When free machining it is advisable to have only a few basic guidelines marked on the fabric so that you can work spontaneously to gradually build up textures and patterns to fill an area. Always experiment on a spare piece of fabric. Depending on the project, it is usually advisable to mount the fabric on to a light-weight cotton backing and machine through both layers. Choose a shallow wooden or metal circular embroidery frame about 15 or 20cm (6 or 8in) with an adjustable screw. The inner ring of the frame should be bound with bias tape which not only holds the fabric securely but also helps to prevent marking the fabric or spoiling previously worked areas should it be necessary to move the frame.

GROWTH AND FORM (DETAIL) BY BARBARA WALTERS.
*Free machining on hand dyed silk and muslin with
applied organzas inspired by basic shapes found in
nature*

1 With a chalk penciol or water-soluble fabric
pen, mark the design lightly on the top fabric, if
necessary, and tack the top fabric to the
backing fabric around the perimeter.

2 Mount the fabric in the frame so that the
design is uppermost on the inside of the inner
ring. Make sure that the grain lines are running
straight in both directions and that the fabric is
taut. Tighten the screw and ease the inner ring
so that it stands slightly proud of the outer one
and the underneath surface is lying flat on the
machine table when working.

Using a frame

1 Thread up the machine in the usual way. Set
the stitch width and length to 0. Check the
tension to ascertain that the top thread runs
freely when pulled through the needle. Remove
the presser foot and lower the feed.

2 Position the frame with the fabric under the
needle and lower the presser foot lever. Bring
both threads to the surface, insert the needle
and hold the threads taut with your left hand
whilst working a few stitches.

3 Place your hands with the fingers on the
edge of the frame and begin to stitch. Maintain
a fairly fast regular speed, whilst moving the
frame smoothly in any direction. Be careful not
to jerk the frame or the needle may break.

Using a darning foot

Mount the work on a backing fabric and prepare the machine as above, with the darning foot attached and the feed lowered. Place the unframed fabric under the darning foot, lower the presser foot lever and stitch as above.

Free-style zigzag

This stitch is useful for filling shapes with solid stitchery or for working grasses and vegetation. You can also work satin stitch 'beads' by machining several stitches on the same spot. Prepare the fabric as above and either remove the foot and frame up the work or attach the darning foot. Set the stitch width to wide, lower the presser foot lever and begin to stitch, moving the fabric or frame from side to side to produce long stitches.

Whip stitch

This is a corded effect with the lower thread whipping and covering the top thread. It is made by altering the tensions of both the top and bottom threads (see page 76). You will need to experiment to achieve the correct relationship between the two.

Whip stitch surrounds the more heavily textured cable stitch

1 Frame up the fabric very tightly or attach a darning foot.

2 Thread up a firm sewing cotton and tighten the top tension as much as necessary. In the bobbin use a fine machine embroidery thread and adjust the bottom tension as necessary.

3 Lower the presser foot lever. Machine quickly and move the frame slowly so that the lower thread comes to the surface and covers the top thread.

Feather stitch

This is a variation on whip stitch with the delicate feathery effect achieved by working in a circular or looping motion. Work as for whip stitch but tighten the top tension to maximum and decrease the lower tension to minimum.

Cable stitch

This is a textured stitch made by winding thick threads such as pearl cotton or knitting yarn on to the bobbin and working from the reverse side of the work.

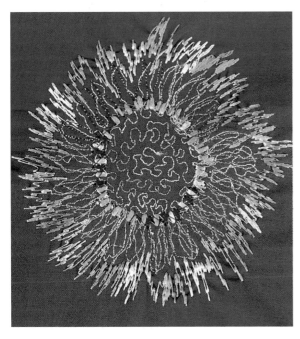

Vermicelli stitch in the centre, outlined with satin stitch beads together with free machining and freestyle zigzag

The circular shape of this flower motif is ideal for feather stitch

1 Draw the design in reverse on the underside of the fabric or the backing and mount the work so that the design is visible when machining.

2 Thread the machine with a normal machine thread on top and wind the bobbin with the thick yarn. This can be done by hand or you can guide the thread through the winding mechanism so that it winds evenly on the bobbin.

3 Loosen the bottom tension so that the thick yarn runs through smoothly and adjust the top tension if necessary.

4 Bring the thick thread to the surface of the framed fabric by threading it in a needle. Straight stitch in the normal way moving the frame so that the lower thicker thread is couched to the underside. If the frame is moved slowly the thicker thread will be completedly covered to give a corded line.

Using Dissolvable Fabrics

The manufacture of hot- and cold-water dissolvable fabrics has opened up a whole range of different effects and possibilities for the machine embroiderer. Both types of dissolvable fabric have certain advantages and you can experiment to see which you prefer. You can produce small lace motifs such as leaves and flowers suitable for decorating clothes and adding to fabric pictures, or you can make whole structures or areas of lacy fabric for wall hangings and other decorative pieces. Freestanding items can be moulded into shape before they are dry and either stitched to a background or used as three-dimensional pieces. Edgings and inserts can be made by tacking a fabric to the dissolvable fabric and stitching heavily along and over the edge to make the lace.

Hot-water dissolvable fabric

This is a fine-woven pale blue fabric which can be stretched taut in a frame. When the embroidery is complete, place it in a pan of boiling water for a few minutes. It will shrivel up as the dissolving takes place, but you can ease it back into shape and pin it out to dry. Tack the embroidery onto a piece of fine cotton before immersion if you prefer, and stretch this instead.

Cold-water dissolvable fabric

This is a white stretchy plastic so it cannot be framed up as taut as the hot-water variety. It also has a tendency to tear when stitched heavily, but you can overcome this by adding another piece beneath the hole. It does dissolve easily in cold water and will not shrivel up.

Stitching

1 Mark the outline of the design on the dissolvable fabric and mount it in a frame.

2 Set up the machine for free machining (see page 81) with the stitch length and width set to minimum. Thread up the top and bobbin with machine embroidery threads.

3 Outline the marked design with several rows of straight stitch machining so that the rows overlap and interlock. The lace will not hold together unless you do this thoroughly.

FANTASY GARDEN BY DIANA DOLMAN. *Machine-made lace fan shapes worked on dissolvable fabric in a variety of threads*

4 Fill in between and over the outlines with a network of interconnecting lines of stitches. For a solid effect fill the area with stitches in several directions.

Dissolving the fabric

When the stitching is complete, cut away as much of the dissolvable fabric as possible before immersion. The stiffness of the machine-made lace will depend on the length of time it has been immersed and also on the thickness of the stitching.

Finishing

Ease the lace into shape or pin it out to dry on a towel. For three-dimensional pieces you can pull or mould it into shape. Small containers can be made by pressing the lace over the bottom of a bottle or bowl. For more rigidity spray-on starch, roller-blind stiffener or a weak solution of PVA adhesive can be applied.

Machine-made lace flowers and trellis are superimposed on a painted background

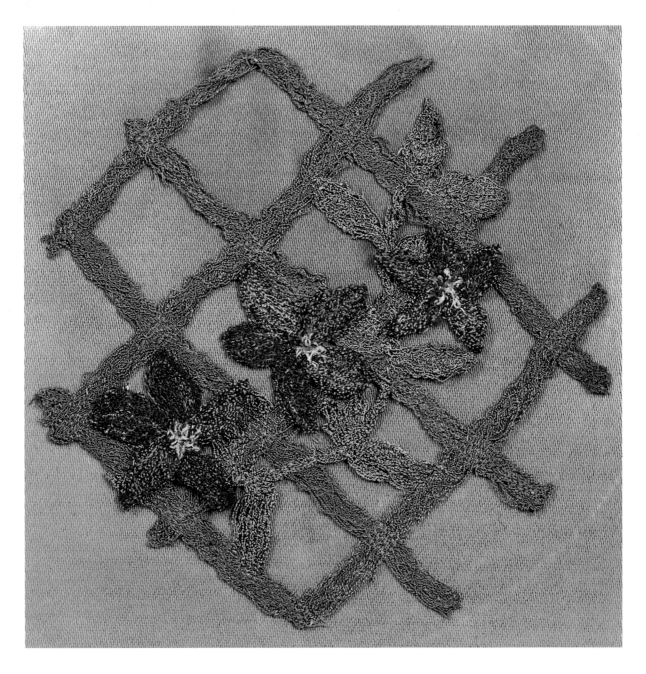

APPLIQUÉ

Appliqué in its basic form is the stitching of different materials to a background fabric. It can be free-style and random with abstract ideas interpreted in different types of fabric and thread, or precise and formal with designs based on geometric shapes, natural forms or everyday objects or motifs.

One of the advantages of appliqué is that it is relatively quick to do. Large areas of colour can be stitched down, giving an instant effect, particularly if you use some of the bonding techniques and a sewing machine. Stitching by hand may take a little longer, but you can achieve individuality with decorative stitches.

The versatility of appliqué is such that it can be used for all manner of different articles from pictures, decorative panels and wall hangings to soft furnishings and clothing. Although it is usually preferable to design and make an article in its entirety, you can easily add a motif or pattern to a ready-made cushion or garment.

There are several appliqué techniques to choose from, each with its own characteristics and potentialities. These can be used in the traditional way or adapted, extended or modified with innovative results. Appliqué can be precise and immaculate, with every part of the design pre-planned, or spontaneous – selecting and cutting different fabrics before stitching them to a plain, painted or dyed background. Bonded appliqué is particularly quick and the effect is immaculate, while the padded and three-dimensional methods can be developed into attractive, textured designs.

'THE LONGEST DAY' ELSPETH KEMP (Detail).
A multimedia work using hand and machine appliqué, stitchery, fabric paints and oil paint sticks (photo by Barry Gould)

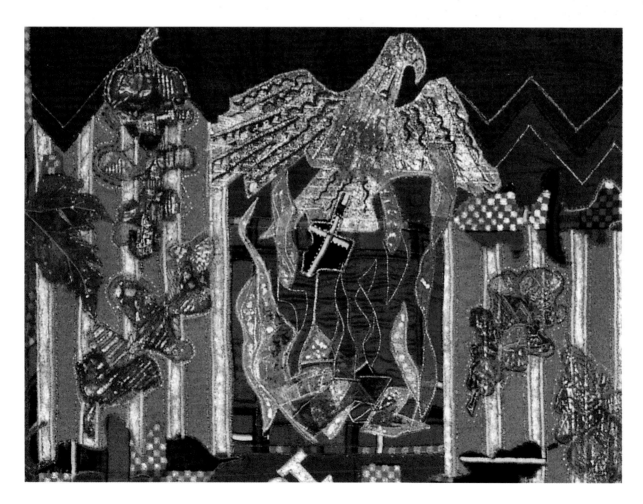

Traditionally it was advisable to align the grain lines, i.e. the warp and weft, of the appliqué patch with that of the background fabric. This is still necessary for projects such as garments or wall hangings which need to drape or hang well. The use of interfacings has largely overcome this necessity especially if you wish to place the patch in a certain direction to give a particular effect. Most hand appliqué projects will benefit from being mounted in either a rectangular embroidery frame or circular hoop whilst you are stitching.

Fabrics

Most fabrics are suitable for appliqué. If the piece is to be purely decorative, then the fabrics can be chosen for their visual impact and texture, if you are decorating clothing or soft furnishings you will need to take their durability and laundering properties into consideration.

Cotton fabrics, including calico, poplin, lawn, voile, corduroy, denim and other firmly woven cotton, are all suitable for backgrounds or for appliqué patches. Depending on their thickness they can be used for most techniques. Except on large-scale designs, you may not be able to turn under the edges on the thicker types such as corduroy and denim, but these can be stitched down with machine zigzag or satin stitches. Dress-weight cotton is ideal for traditional appliqué as the edges will turn crisply and you can stitch by hand or machine. Sheer fabrics such as voiles and nets can be torn, ruched or gathered and stitched randomly by hand or machine.

Silk fabrics range from chunky tweed to fine Honan; most wash well and can be painted or dyed with beautiful results. Silk chiffon and organza can be treated in a similar way to the cotton transparent fabrics above.

Wool fabrics are not traditionally used for appliqué but they have a lovely soft feel and look which may be appropriate for a project.

Facing page: ANNA CHRISTY 'MONEMVASIA' (DETAIL). *Layers of raw-edged gauzes and other fabrics are held in place with hand and machine stitches*

Tweeds are often patterned or textured and can provide their own kind of inspiration. Printed wool challis may have a design with motifs which can be cut out and then stitched to a contrasting background.

Synthetic fibres range from polyester and nylon, to acrylic and rayon and are usually washable. Although some may have a springy quality which makes turning a crisp edge difficult, they are ideal for machine or bonded appliqué on clothing or soft furnishings.

Non-woven fabrics include felt, interfacing, leather and suede. All these are easy to use as they do not fray or stretch. As they have no grain direction they can simply be cut out and stitched at will. Suede, leather and interfacing can also be painted or dyed.

Knitted fabrics such as jersey are rather difficult to handle as backgrounds unless they are mounted on a backing, but their stretchy quality makes them ideal for manipulating into gathers or scrunching up into interesting textures for a decorative panel.

For experimental pieces, you may like to try stitching different types of paper and plastics. These can be manipulated into pleats, painted, dyed, gathered or crumpled for exciting results.

Although appliqué patches were not backed in the past, iron-on interfacings and bonding web are often used today and extend the potential of a number of techniques.

Threads

Most appliqué techniques, whether by hand or machine, require cotton or polyester sewing cotton, which either matches or contrasts with the appliqué patch. Although it is the generally accepted practice to sew cotton with cotton and synthetic with synthetic, this is not absolutely necessary, though you may wish to buy silk thread for a silk project in order to match the lustres. If you are intending to embroider the appliqué, you can use any of the usual embroidery threads such as stranded or pearl cotton, together with knitting, crochet or tapestry yarns. Choose a needle appropriate in size to the fabric and thread.

Interfacings

Although not traditionally used for appliqué, interfacings, including the iron-on type and bonding web, are invaluable for backing the fabric patches for some methods. They give a crisp durable finish, although they make the result a little stiffer.

Iron-on interfacing is available in a wide range of thicknesses and qualities: your choice will depend on the fabric being used and the effect you wish to create. Light-weight interfacing will support fine fabrics, while heavier types give a stiff result. An added advantage is that when fine fabrics are backed in this way, the edge of the shape or motif can be well-defined and the seam allowance will not show through. Fabrics which fray or those which are slippery or difficult to handle can be stabilized by being suported with a well chosen interfacing.

1 Place the interfacing, shiny side up over the design and trace using a pencil or fabric marker. Mark the grain line, if necessary, on the other (non-adhesive) side. Cut out the shape on the marked line.

Marking the design on the reverse shiny side of the interfacing

2 Place the shape, shiny side down on the reverse side of the appliqué fabric, aligning the grain if necessary. Press with a steam iron, set to the appropriate setting.

3 Cut out the shape, either with turnings for turned-edge appliqué or without if the interfacing is being used simply as a support for raw-edge appliqué.

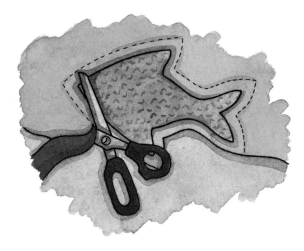

Cutting out the ironed on motif in appliqué fabric for turned-edge appliqué

Bonding web

Bonding web is a paper-backed, double-sided adhesive web, which bonds fabrics together when ironed and lessens their fraying qualities. It is particularly useful for machine appliqué, for Persian appliqué, for the random placement of fabric patches and for the creation of three dimensional motifs. You can also make fabric beads with it (see page 109) or use it to hold hems or ribbons in place before you begin stitching (see page 112).

1 Trace the design in reverse. Position the bonding web smooth side up on top and trace the design to make a reverse image. Mark the grain line on the smooth side

2 Cut out the shape allowing a margin all round and place it rough side down on the reverse side of the fabric, matching grain lines if necessary. Iron with as hot an iron as the fabric will allow.

3 When cool, cut out the shape on the marked lines through the fabric and the backing paper. Peel off the backing paper.

Sample with bonded lettering attached with machine zigzag

4 Position the shape on the background and iron firmly ready for stitching.

5 To make sure that the bonding web does not stick to your iron place a sheet of baking parchment or silicone paper on top and iron through this. This is particularly necessary when bonding sheer fabrics such as net, nylon and organza.

Appliqué Techniques

Raw-edged appliqué
This is one of the simplest appliqué methods, as the fabric shapes are cut out and stitched without turnings. Non-woven fabrics, such as felt, leather, suede, net and painted interfacings, which do not fray, can be cut and applied, either with invisible stitches, decorative embroidery stitches or by machine. Synthetic fabrics which normally fray can have their edges singed with a hot stencil cutter or soldering

iron. This method needs to be done with extreme care. You should make small experiments first and work in a well ventilated room as some fabrics emit noxious fumes. If you are working on a large project you are advised to wear a mask and respirator. Mark the shapes on the fabric and mount it in an embroidery frame. Draw the hot tool slowly along the marked lines to cut out the shapes.

There are several products on the market which act like a glue to seal the edges of fabric. These are suitable for appliqué on panels, pictures and articles which will be not subjected to hard wear. Apply the glue in tiny dots or elongated dots similar to stitches for the best effect.

For a formal appliqué project, make a tracing of the design, cut out the pattern pieces and use these as a guide for cutting the fabric. Then assemble the fabric patches in a logical order, overlapping them as necessary. Begin with those in the background and superimpose the foreground shapes.

RAW-EDGED APPLIQUÉ COCKEREL BY ANNA GRIFFITHS.
Felt is an ideal fabric for raw-edged appliqué stitched with free machining

Persian appliqué

Persian appliqué is a raw-edged method which was developed as an imitation of embroidery, with motifs such as flowers and birds cut from printed cotton and stitched to a background. Today the simplest way of approaching this method is to iron a sheet of bonding web to the back of the printed fabric prior to cutting out the motifs. These can then be arranged and ironed in place. Secure the edges with slip stitches or tiny buttonhole stitches. If you prefer to work by machine, use either a narrow zigzag, satin or an automatic embroidery stitch.

A transparent appliqué foot or an open-fronted foot will help you to see the edge of the fabric clearly. For the stitching to be a prominent feature, choose a sewing cotton which contrasts with the background and the appliqué motifs; if you wish it to be hardly noticeable stitch either with a cotton which matches the motifs or an invisible machine thread.

YVONNE MORTON 'AKETON' (DETAIL). *Layers of organzas and metallic fabrics are cut away using the reverse-appliqué technique*

Random appliqué

A spontaneous abstract approach can be carried out successfully both by beginners and the more experienced. Cut, torn or singed pieces of fabric are given different shapes and stitched by hand or machine to the background fabric to make an innovative texture which could be the basis for further appliqué, embroidery, painting, or beadwork. If you are using bonding web, iron large pieces to a several squares of different fabrics, cut out random shapes and position them ready for bonding. Transparent fabrics and those which have been painted or dyed are particularly effective; they can be overlapped, placed in regular patterns or scattered across the surface.

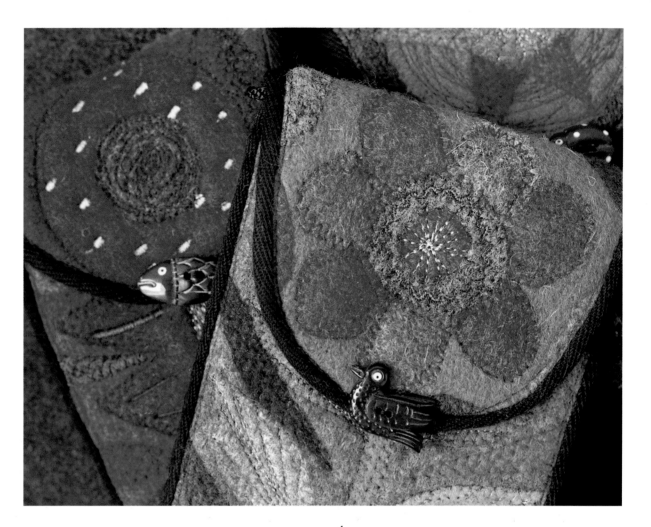

APPLIQUÉD PURSES BY TERESA SEARLE. *Machine knitted felted wool acts as a background fabric for this group of purses with appliqué flowers in the same fabric. Machine embroidered with details worked by hand (photographed by Nigel Currivan)*

Turned-edge appliqué

Also known as blind appliqué, this hand method is probably the most popular, particularly for appliqué quilts, for fabrics which fray and for the padded methods. It results in a smooth-edged effect which needs no additional decoration, although you can add embroidery if you wish. The patches can be backed with iron-on interfacing (see page 90), and they are cut out with a seam allowance which is then turned under before you begin stitching to the background, either with unobtrusive slip stitches or a decorative version such as buttonhole.

1 If you are using iron on interfacing, follow the instructions for this, making sure to add a turning of between 6mm (¼in) and 12mm (½in)

Cutting out the motif allowing turnings

depending on the size and intricacy of the shape. Alternatively use a tracing of the design, marking vertical grain lines and number each piece if necessary. Cut out the pattern pieces and use these as a guide for cutting the fabric, aligning the grain with the marked lines and adding the turnings.

2 Fold over the turning to the reverse side, snipping curves and trimming excess fabric from the corners. Tack the turning in place with the knot on the right side.

Folding over turnings and tacking in place

3 Pin and tack the prepared patch in place. Secure with slip stitch. Bring the needle up through the background fabric close to the edge of the patch and take a tiny stitch into the turned edge, at right angles to the edge. Repeat at 6mm (¼in) intervals. Remove both sets of tacking stitches.

Stitching the motif to the background

Padded Appliqué

Using a variety of paddings to raise the surface of appliqué patches gives another dimension to a project. It can be used for a softly textured effect or a sculptured surface in high or low relief. The choice of padding will depend on the desired effect. You can use layers of felt which give a firm surface, soft synthetic wadding which allows stitchery to be worked through it for a quilted effect, or stiff card or craft interfacing which is ideal for hard-edged designs such as architectural or geometric subjects. An innovative idea is to use transparent fabric covering small snippets of fabric or beads trapped beneath the surface.

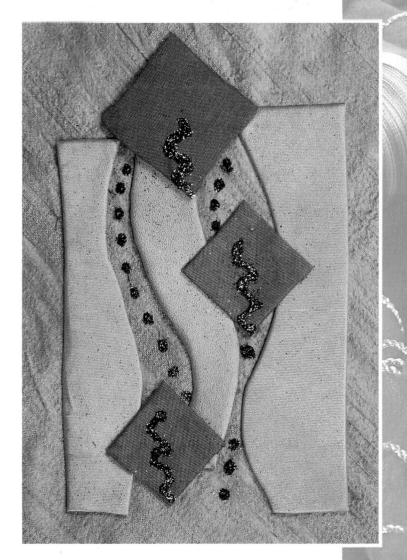

Padded appliqué

Padding with felt

1 Cut a piece of felt the same shape and size as the appliqué patch. Then cut two or three more, each slightly smaller than the last.

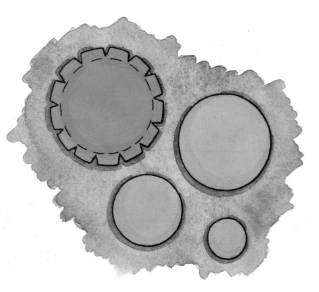

Preparing appliqué patch and similar shapes in felt

2 Using small slip stitches at right angles to the edge, stitch the smallest piece of felt in the centre of the area to be padded. Cover this with the next size and continue until each piece is stitched securely.

Stitching the felt shapes in ascending order

3 Stitch the turned-edge appliqué patch on top. This will result in a firm domed shape.

4 The padding can be stitched off-centre, but you may need to adjust the shape of the appliqué patch to eliminate wrinkles.

Padding with wadding

1 Cut a piece of synthetic wadding the same shape and size as the appliqué patch and stitch it down with small loose straight stitches at right-angles to the edge.

2 Stitch the turned-edge appliqué patch on top.

Stitching the wadding to the background and preparing appliqué patch

Padding with card or craft interfacing

1 Cut a piece of card or interfacing the same size and shape as the finished appliqué shape.

2 Iron a piece of bonding web to the appliqué fabric and cut out the patch adding turnings. Remove the paper backing.

3 Place the fabric patch centrally over the card or interfacing and iron with the iron set to the appropriate setting.

4 Turn over so that the card is uppermost. Snip any curves to within 3mm (⅛in) of the edge of the card and trim excess fabric from the corners.

Cutting card or interfacing and preparing appliqué patch

5 With the tip of the iron, press the turnings down on to the back of the card.

Pressing the turnings over the edge of the card or interfacing

6 Slip stitch or stick the appliqué patch to the background.

Entrapping

1 Prepare the appliqué patch either with raw edges or turnings in transparent fabric such as net, organza or nylon.

2 The seeds, beads, sequins or snippets of fabric can either be stitched in place before adding the appliqué or can float freely. If you decide on the latter, stitch round the appliqué patch, leaving a small gap through which to insert the tiny items. Carefully push them through the gap, using a funnel if the shape is large, and then stitch up the gap to secure.

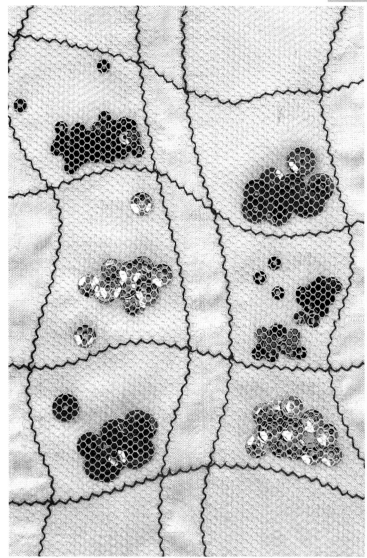

A layer of machine-stitched net entraps a selection of sequins

Three-dimensional Appliqué

Decorative panels and pictures often have raised motifs such as leaves and flowers projecting from the surface. They are usually attached with a few firm stitches to hold them in place. They can be made with two layers of fabric bonded together or be stuffed with felt or wadding, depending on the effect needed. Florist's or fuse wire stitched to the motif will enable it to be manipulated or the whole can be sprayed with roller-blind stiffener or painted with a weak solution of fabric adhesive.

WEDDING DRESS (DETAIL) BY AVRIL LANSDELL *showing three-dimensional appliqué leaves and flowers*

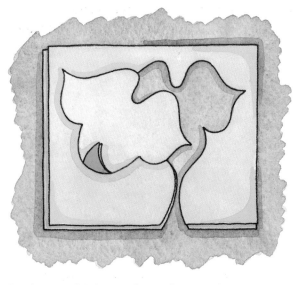

Bonding two fabrics together and cutting them out

Flat-bonded motifs

1 Bond two similar or contrasting fabrics together with bonding web. Mark the design and cut out.

2 The edges can be left plain or covered with hand embroidery. If you wish to use a machine satin stitch, work this prior to cutting out. It is often easier to treat details such as leaf veins or flower centres in a similar way.

3 For motifs which need to be moulded to a specific shape, place a length of fine florist's wire between the two layers before bonding. This can be oversewn by hand or machine or left unadorned.

4 To stiffen the work use roller-blind spray and work out of doors or by an open window. As an alternative PVA adhesive diluted with two or three parts water can be painted on to the motif to stiffen it and mould it into shape.

Padded raw-edged motifs

1 Mark the shape on the right side of a piece of top fabric and place it on a piece of bottom fabric with a thin layer of synthetic wadding between. Tack the layers together and finish with a machined line of stitching just inside the marked line. Remove the tacking.

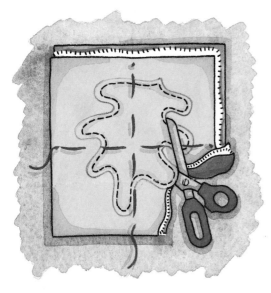

Assembling the layers, stitching and cutting out

2 Cut out the motif close to the stitching and work a narrow open zigzag or satin stitch over the edge, using a transparent appliqué foot. If you prefer to work by hand, stitch the layers together with tiny running stitches and finish with close buttonhole stitch or overcasting. Details can be added by hand or machine.

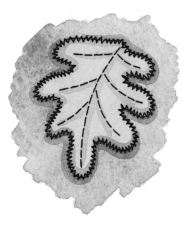

Machine stitching the edges and details

Turned-through motifs

1 Mark the shape on the reverse side of a piece of top fabric. Tack the pieces of top and bottom fabrics right sides together with the wadding beneath.

2 Machine stitch (or running stitch) along the marked line. Cut a small diagonal slit in the centre of the bottom fabric, through which to turn the work.

3 Remove the tacking and cut out the motif, trimming the wadding close to the seam. Snip any curves and trim excess fabric from corners.

Assembling the layers, cutting out and slitting

4 Turn the motif through to the right side. Press lightly and oversew the opening. Finish the edge and any details with top stitching. Decorative stitching can be an alternative finish.

Turning through to the right side and finishing with top stitching

BEADS, SEQUINS, JEWELS AND FOUND OBJECTS

'ANENOME MASK' (DETAIL) BY DIANA DOLMAN. *Painted silk, machine embroidered and hand stitched with beads and semi-precious stone chips*

The addition of any small three-dimensional object to plain, painted or dyed fabric will give a highly textured surface. The effect can be theatrical or ethnic, depending on the materials that you use. Beading, sequins and jewels can give a luxurious look to your evening garments and accessories, while wooden beads and found objects such as feathers, driftwood or metal items can be incorporated in decorative embroidered panels or wall hangings.

Beadwork

Beads come in many different guises, from the tiniest seed pearls and glass spheres, known as rocailles, to large-scale versions in wood, plastic, metal or china. They may be faceted or smooth, round, cuboid, or tubular; long beads are known as bugles and there are pendant shapes such as teardrops. You can fashion your own beads from clay, wood, pasta, seeds, leather, fabric, paper or found objects.

Sequins and spangles are available in different colours and shapes, the most usual being cup- or disc-shaped with a central hole. Specialist shops also stock sequins in the form of leaves, flowers, shells, stars and geometric shapes. Wide strips of sequin waste (from which sequins have been punched during manufacture) is a useful acquisition as it can be cut up into small pieces and stitched to form patterns or texture. Avoid the temptation to use it in large pieces because the effect can be rather unattractive.

Embroidery stones and jewels come in a wide colour and size range and in various shapes from circular, square, lozenge and pendant. Most have a flat underside and are pierced with holes for attaching to fabric. Those without holes can be glued to the fabric surface or attached with covering stitches. Shisha (or mirror) glass and metal discs or coins are traditionally sewn with a type of buttonhole stitch around the edge.

The most successful beaded designs are those where the beads or sequins are massed together to form a sold texture or the focal point of a piece. They can be scattered delicately across the surface of the fabric with the number gradually diminishing, or used in formal patterns as a border or a pretty edging.

It is essential that the background fabric for beading is mounted in an embroidery frame. Choose a fabric which is firmly woven and if necessary back it with a supporting material. Fine fabrics such as chiffon or organza can be backed with a fabric which is cut away when the beading is completed. Alternatively, a water dissolvable fabric can be used as a backing which will disappear when plunged into water when you have completed the design. If using this method, remember to work in a logical way as the stitches underneath will be visible, if the beads have spaces between them.

Beading needles which are extremely fine and long are available from specialist shops, or you can use any fine needle which will go through the holes in the beads or sequins. Use strong thread which can be further strengthened and kept straight by drawing it through a block of beeswax.

Single and pairs of beads

Secure single or pairs of beads with a single stitch through the hole or both holes. A large bead can be attached by using a smaller one on top. Bring the thread up through both beads and down again through the one nearest the surface of the fabric. Secure firmly with a double back stitch in the backing fabric.

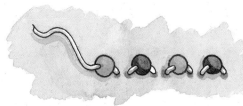

Attaching single beads

Attaching pairs of beads

Attaching one bead with another

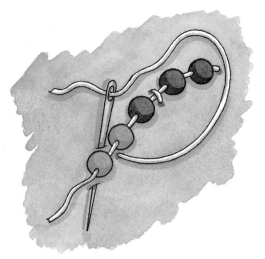

Couching beads

Couching beads

Rows of beads can be couched down in lines, spirals or outlines. Bring the thread to the surface of the fabric and thread on the required number of beads, laying them along the line of the design. Using a second needle and thread, take a tiny stitch across the row of beads, between each bead or every two or three, depending on the complexity of the design, and the size of the beads. Finish by bringing both threads to the back of the work and fastening off securely.

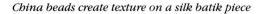

China beads create texture on a silk batik piece

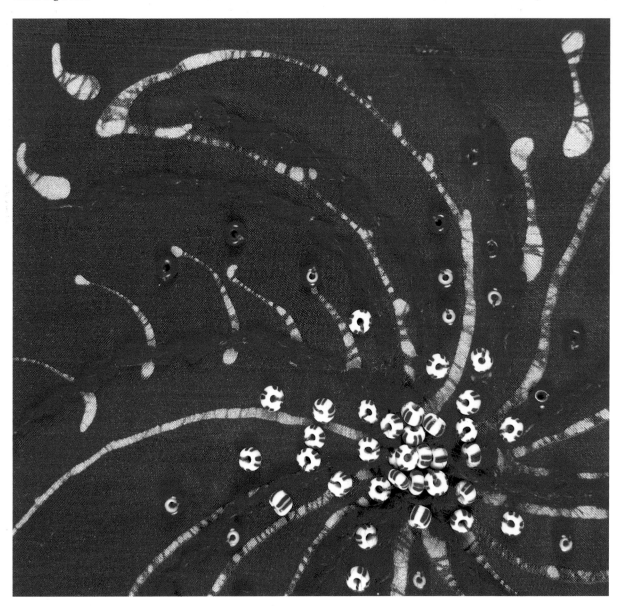

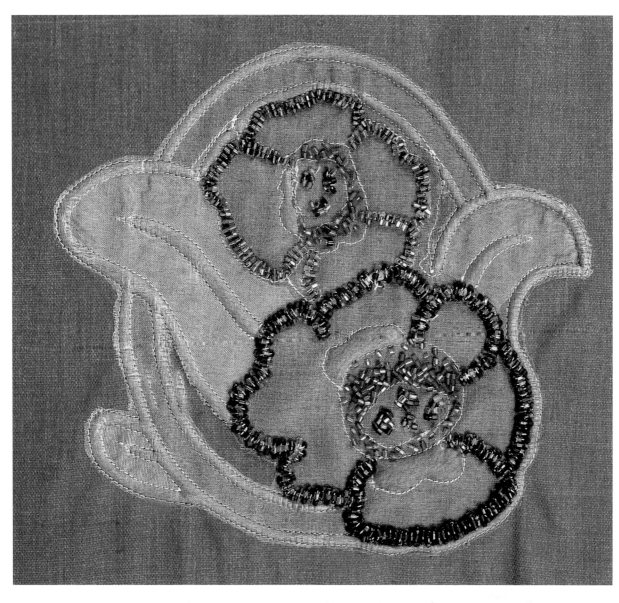

Tiny glass beads are attached singly, in pairs and over a cord to emphasize the overlay of organza

Beading over a cord

For a raised linear beaded effect, couch a cord on to the background fabric following the line of the design. Bring a second thread to the surface one side of the cord, thread on three or four beads, equal to the width of the cord. Insert the needle on the opposite side of the cord, either straight across or diagonally. Repeat the process, covering the cord with beads. This method can be varied by leaving gaps between the rows of beads or, alternatively, by choosing the colours to produce a diagonal or lengthwise striped pattern.

Beading over a cord

Making a loop

A sampler showing beads, jewels and sequins attached in a variety of ways

Bead loops and fringes

To sew a loop, bring the thread to the surface, thread on an uneven number of beads and re-insert the needle back into the fabric at almost the same point from which it emerged.

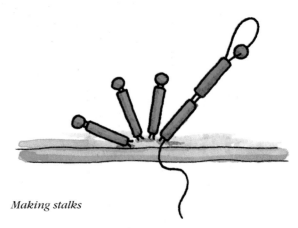

Making stalks

Stalks can be made by threading several beads and taking the needle back again through all except the top bead. Fringes and tassels can be fashioned in a similar way using any number of beads. These can be arranged in such a way as to produce a chevron, striped or similar pattern.

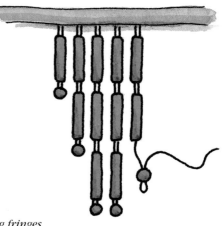

Making fringes

Attaching Sequins

Individual sequins can be sewn with two, three or four stitches radiating from the central hole, or they can be held in place by a small bead. A line of sequins or flat spangles can be secured with back stitches, so that the sequins overlap and the stitches are invisible.

'ELIZABETHAN FANTASY' (DETAIL) BY AVRIL LANSDELL.
Appliqué flowers with massed beadwork

Attaching sequins with a bead or stitches

Attaching a row of sequins with back stitch

Attaching Jewels and Stones

These make a strong statement or focal point. Although some flat-backed artificial jewels and stones have holes for stitching, others will need to be attached in some other way. They can be glued in place or sewn with a lattice work of needlelace stitches, with buttonhole stitch or a ring of felt, suede or leather around the edge. If you use spider's web stitch (see page 67) you will need to interweave the base stitches unless there is a hole in the centre of the jewel.

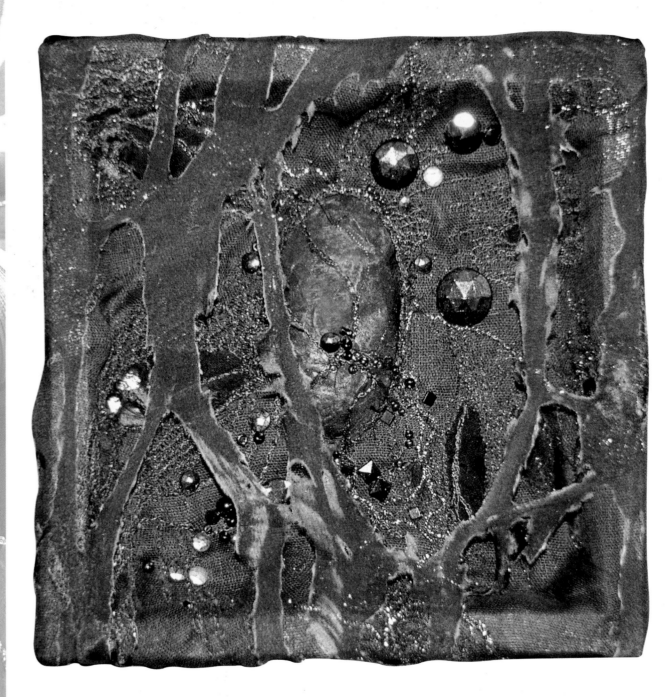

'BEFORE CREATION' BY BARBARA WALTERS. *Machine and hand embroidery with added jewels, beads and buttons, mounted on a box*

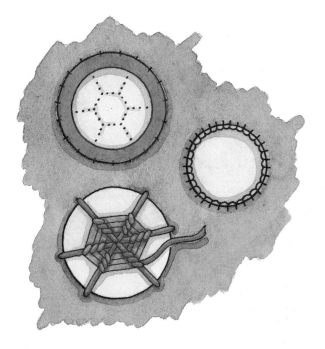

Attaching jewels with a circle of suede, leather or felt; detached buttonhole stitch; and spider's web stitch

Detail of a panel by Margaret Griffiths with glass, jewels and buttons attached with shisha stitch

Attaching Shisha Glass and Coins

1 Secure the shisha glass or coin with a small dab of glue. Using an embroidery thread make two parallel horizontal stitches across the surface. Bring the needle out at the top and work two vertical stitches, each time passing over and under each horizontal thread.

2 Bring the needle out at the edge of the glass and take it over the intersecting threads. Make a small stitch close to the edge, pulling the thread tight and bringing the needle through the loop. Repeat, going over the central framework and work in a clockwise direction until the edge of the glass is completely covered. Fasten off securely.

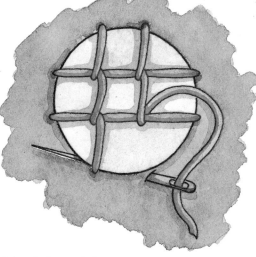

Working the base stitches

Working the edge stitches

Dyeing Beads and Pearls

Although there are many different coloured beads on the market, you may not be able to find exactly the right shade. To colour glass beads and pearls you will need French enamel varnish which is available from specialist shops. The colours are intermixable and can be diluted with methylated spirits. Simply dip the string of beads in the solution and hang up to drip dry. If the beads are already stitched to the background fabric they can be painted individually with a cotton bud dipped in the varnish. Should you wish to spray them, do remember to mask off those areas which you do not wish to colour. Pearl beads can be coloured by dipping them in hot water dyes (see page 40).

Making Your Own Beads

Paper beads

For this type of handmade bead you can use plain coloured craft paper, scraps of wallpaper, wrapping paper, magazine cuttings or paper which you have decorated with paint, dyes, markers or crayons. Computer printouts on paper or paper-backed silk are another option to consider.

1 Cut long elongated triangles from the paper and roll each one round a knitting needle, fine pencil or cocktail stick, starting at the wider end. Secure the points with a dab of glue, remove from the needle and leave to dry. This will result in an oval shaped bead. You can experiment by rolling different shapes of paper – you will find that shorter wide triangles will result in round beads, while straight lengths will result in cylindrical shapes.

2 If you wish to varnish or decorate the beads further, thread them back on the needle and implant them in a knob of plasticine or clay while painting.

A selection of hand-made beads in paper, felt, leather and polymer clay

Fabric beads

Pelmet or craft interfacing, felt, leather, suede and all sorts of other fabrics can be fashioned into beads in a similar way to those in paper. You can either use fabric glue or iron bonding web on to the back of the fabric, then cut the triangles to shape, tear off the paper backing and roll up around the knitting needle. Secure your work with a pin, and iron gently through a sheet of baking parchment. For a decorative edge work narrow machine, zigzag before cutting out the triangles or embellish the rolls with fabric paint, stitched beads or sequins. Small circles of the above thick non-fray fabrics can also be coloured and cut into tiny sequin shapes which can then be attached with a tiny stitch or a bead.

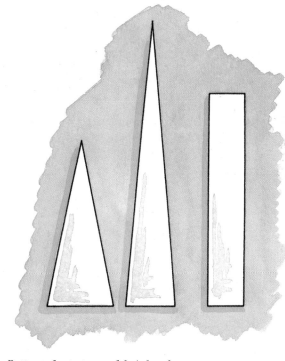

Patterns for paper or fabric beads

Clay beads

There are several polymer clays on the market, some of which are self-hardening whilst others can be baked in an ordinary oven. They come in a wide range of intermixable colours, but they can also be painted, highlighted with gold leaf, sprayed or impressed with a sharp tool or with textured fabrics such as lace or hessian. The shape of the beads you use can vary from conventional tubular or spherical types to motifs such as flowers or leaves, which can all be decorated as above.

1 Roll out the clay into a long sausage shape; cut straight or diagonally across and pierce each bead using a knitting needle or cocktail stick.

2 For square, rectangular or triangular beads, form the 'sausage' into the appropriate shaped length, by flattening the sides with a piece of wood. Cut into lengths and pierce the holes as before. Round beads can be made by rolling the clay into tiny balls and piercing as before.

3 Leave to dry or bake according to the manufacturers' instructions.

4 Decorate in your chosen way and seal the surface with varnish or shellac.

Seed beads

Various seeds, such as those from melons, sunflowers and pumpkins make unusual beads. Allow them to dry naturally or place them on a baking tray in a low oven for an hour or two. Holes can then be drilled using a hand-drill fitted with a very fine bit. Some seeds already have beautiful natural colours or they can be painted or varnished. Dried pulses such as beans and peas can be treated in a similar way. Depending on their shape and size, all these can be stitched in the conventional way, or glued in place.

Found materials

Besides seeds and pulses, the natural world will provide you with a wealth of different things which can be used as types of bead. Shells, bamboo, tiny pieces of driftwood or bone all make interesting decorative elements if used in a sensitive way. Pasta, such as macaroni or any other type with a hole, can be varnished or painted. Hardware shops can be worth exploring for metal nuts, rings, plastic tube and all sorts of other items which can be converted by painting or overcasting with thread.

You may need to use your imagination when dealing with some of these items. Try to transform them so that even on close inspection they do not resemble the original. Some can be attached in the normal way with a stitch through the hole or sewn using the methods described above for jewels and shisha glass. Irregularly shaped items without holes may need needleweaving to hold them:

Working needleweaving over found objects

1 If possible stick the object to the background with a dab of glue. Take a number of radiating or criss-crossing stitches across the object to hold it in place.

2 Bring the needle to the surface at the starting point and work weaving stitches as for woven wheels (see page 66) across the base stitches until the object is held firmly in place.

3 If you wish, repeat with another area of needleweaving crossing the first.

4 Alternatively you can work a series of base stitches crisscrossing the object and then work spider's web stitch (see page 67) to hold it.

5 Depending on the shape of the found object, you may be able to work shisha stitch (see page 107) to hold it firm.

RIBBONS, BRAIDS AND CORDS

Ribbons and lace are the classic embellishment for pretty clothing and accessories, from bridal and evening wear to delicate items for the nursery. Purchased cushions, table and bed linen can all be given individuality by adding some well-chosen decoration. Tassels, braids, pompoms, cords and fringes are the traditional way of decorating soft furnishing items and can be purchased or handmade in a variety of dif- ferent yarns. They can also be added to garments or decorative wall hangings. For added embellishment you can incorporate beads or colour them with paint or dyes to fit in with your interior design scheme.

Today, there are many different types of ribbons and braids to choose from in a myriad of colours and widths. Ribbons may be plain, woven or printed with patterns, in satin, brocade, sheer organza, velvet, grosgrain or lurex. Most are in synthetic fibres, and they will withstand washing even though they may look

A selection of ribbons

delicate. Silk ribbons are more fragile but are good for using as embroidery threads. Craft ribbons which are meant for gift wrapping and floristry are not washable so should not be used for clothing or soft furnishing. However, they are stiff and shiny, do not fray and are good for experimenting by painting or cutting into shapes for appliqué. Some craft ribbons have wire fused along either one or both edges so they can easily be manipulated into shape. Braids come in wool, cotton or manmade fibres in a variety of patterns and widths.

Applying Ribbons, Braids and Cords

A few simple rules are all that are necessary for successful ribbon appliqué. The simplest and most successful way is to use a sewing machine. Use a fine needle and thread to tack

'BOILED SWEET CUSHION' BY GRETA FITCHETT.
Appliquéd cottons and silks on velvet with gathered ribbons

the ribbon in place. (Try to avoid using pins for satin ribbon as the pin-holes will leave unsightly marks). An alternative is to use bonding web, which is available in narrow widths, to position the ribbon prior to stitching (see page 90). Machine stitch along the right-hand edge of the ribbon, then along the left, always in the same direction. You can use a straight machine stitch or a narrow open zigzag. If you are stitching several rows or one ribbon superimposed on another, always sew them in the same direction.

For velvet ribbons use a zipper foot so as not to crush the pile. Very narrow ribbons can be couched down with a wide open zigzag stitch which crosses the entire width or you can use a twin needle of the appropriate width to stitch both edges in one operation. Another method of machine stitching is to use a braiding foot through which you thread the narrow ribbon so that it is automatically fed through under the zigzag stitches; cords can be couched in a similar way. Plain ribbons can be further embellished by rows of decorative automatic machine stitches on either edge or down the centre. If you prefer to stitch by hand, use tiny running stitches, back stitch or hemstitching.

Decorative Ways With Ribbons, Braids and Cords

Besides simply stitching ribbon in straight lines, you can manipulate it in imaginative ways for different effects. You can gather one edge for a frilled effect or down the centre for a double frill. A length can be pressed into accordian or box pleats, and, by folding and pressing a ribbon into zigzags or triangles, you can form linear or geometric designs to embellish table or bedlinen. Small pieces of ribbon can be fashioned into soft or pleated loops to hang as an edging.

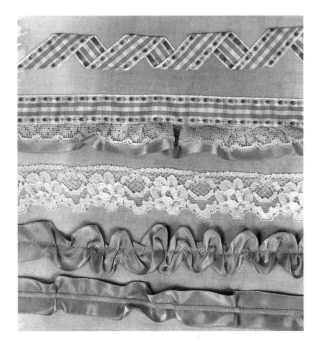

Decorative ideas for stitching ribbons and lace

Shell edging

A strip of shell edging can be used to decorate the hem, collar or cuffs of a blouse or on pretty children's wear such as bridesmaids' dresses. Work a zigzag line of running stitches along a length of ribbon before gathering the stitches to form the shape.

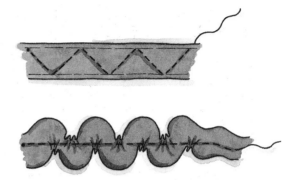

Stitching shell edging and gathering it up

Braids and cords are usually more flexible than ribbons which makes them suitable for applying to curved shapes such as the hem of a garment, a collar or a circular cushion. Curvilinear designs such as spirals and circles can be created and inspiration can be taken by looking at Celtic design. Although braids are traditionally glued to upholstery, for other uses it is generally best to stitch them invisibly by hand or machine.

Making Your Own Ribbons and Braids

Although there is a wealth of ready-made decoration available, it is an interesting prospect to experiment with strips of fabric, handmade plaits, cords and braids to create your own.

Ribbons made out of fabrics

Silk, rayon, muslin, organza or nylon can be torn into strips of varying widths with the frayed edges giving additional texture and interest. If you prefer you can singe the edges of synthetic fibres, with an electric tool such as a hot stencil cutter or soldering iron (see page 12). You can either place ready cut or torn strips in an embroidery frame and singe the edges or you

Decorative fringe incorporating torn fabrics, bias edged strips and rouleaux loops

can frame up a whole piece of fabric and draw the hot tool across the surface to make the strips. These can then be attached in the normal way or by ruching or gathering. For a more rigid solid effect, the edges of strips of fabric can be joined lengthwise with right sides together and turned through to the right side with the seam at centre back.

Rouleaux

Besides traditional fringing, you can make loops or effective hanging ribbons from rouleaux or neatened bias strips. Rouleaux are particularly useful as they can also be used for linear designs or to represent natural forms such as flower stems. They can be plaited together, used for straps on bags or stitched in patterns for openwork designs.

1 Cut a bias strip double the finished width plus a 6mm (¼in) seam allowance on each side.

2 Fold the strip in half lengthwise with right sides together and machine stitch.

3 Using a strong thread and a large needle or bodkin, attach the thread to one end of the fabric strip and then push the needle through, eye forward, back through the strip, pulling it right side out.

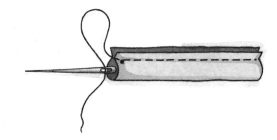

Inserting needle to turn the rouleau

Neatened bias strips in soft fabrics such as silk, net or organza can be used as streamers or loops for the edges of wall hangings, cushions or garments. Cut bias strips in various widths from 12–25mm (½–1in). Neaten the edges by machining with an open zigzag stitch.

Plaits and braids

These are usually heavy in texture and size and can be fashioned with ribbons, threads, strips of fabric or rouleaux. For formal plaits use ribbons or threads of similar size, but for more experimental results try those of different types and widths. Fine ribbons or knitting wools can be knotted and then plaited, rouleaux can be twisted into cords with metallic or embroidery threads. Machine-made cords are easy to make particularly if you have a braiding foot (see 81). Thread up the machine with an interesting yarn such as a metallic or shaded thread. You can then feed heavy embroidery threads, crochet cottons, or knitting yarns under the machine foot and zigzag over them, producing a colourful whipped effect. Experiment with zigzags of different lengths and widths for a variety of effects.

Ribbon Embroidery

This technique was very popular in Victorian times and has recently been re-introduced as a craft now that beautiful narrow silk and satin ribbons are more readily available. Specialist suppliers can provide packs of silk ribbons in co-ordinated colour ranges in 2mm, 4mm and 7mm widths.

Most free-style surface embroidery stitches can be adapted and the effect can be highly textured. French knots, chain stitch, straight stitches, herringbone and feather stitch are particularly effective. Choose a fabric which is fairly loosely woven and mount it with a

Hand dyed ribbon embroidery using a variety of stitches, including Banksia rose stitch, petal stitch and ribbon loops

backing fabric in an embroidery frame. As an alternative you can use needlepoint canvas or a firm evenweave fabric which is made for counted cross stitch (these do not need to be backed). Use a large-eyed needle, big enough to accommodate the ribbon. Starting and finishing can present a few problems and knots should be avoided. With another needle threaded with fine thread secure the ribbon at the back at the starting and finishing points with a few back stitches. The most important aspect to remember is to keep the ribbon from twisting unnecessarily. Before pulling the ribbon tight, loop it over your finger and pull gently to acquire the desired tension.

French knots

French knots are particularly attractive worked in ribbon as the knot stands away from the surface. (see pages 115 and 116). Mass them together for a knobbly texture or use them individually for flower centres.

Detached chain

This is also known as daisy stitch and is often used in a flower shape or for leaves. Individual stitches can be worked randomly over the surface. Bring the needle to the surface and insert it again alongside, leaving a loop. Then bring the needle up through the loop and take a small vertical stitch to hold it, making sure the ribbon does not twist.

Petal stitch

Petal stitch has been developed specially for ribbon embroidery and makes a pretty addition to the repertoire. Bring the ribbon to the surface and lay it along the stitching line. Pierce through the ribbon and the background, bring the needle to the back and making a tiny fold at the end of the stitch. Be careful not to pull the ribbon too tight.

Working petal stitch

Banksia rose stitch

This makes a small pretty round shape. To form the centre of the rose, make three or four French knots or small looped stitches on the surface close together, securing the last one with a back stitch. Then work four stem stitches surrounding the loops. Continue working stem stitch round the shape until the rose is the desired size.

Working detached chain stitch

Working Banksia rose stitch

Working fern stitch

Fern stitch

This stitch is made up of three straight stitches which radiate from a central hole. As the name implies, single stitches are good for foliage or grasses, but it can also be used as a continuous line stitch.

Ribbon Flowers

As ribbons make such a pretty and dainty effect, flowers are often the natural choice for a design. They can be entirely three-dimensional, such as ribbon roses, or more simply have a raised surface as with Banksia rose stitch which emulates the shape and form of the flower.

Three-dimensional ribbon roses

These are the classic decoration for bridal or evening wear, but can also be added to embroidered or appliqué panels, or pretty cushions and covers. Although in theory they can be made of any width, it is best to practice with 50 x 2.5cm (20 x 1in) ribbon.

1 Roll one end of the ribbon into a small tight roll and secure the bottom with a few stitches to form the centre of the rose.

2 Fold the ribbon diagonally away from you, keeping the folded edge slightly above the centre roll. Turn the centre roll towards the fold and stitch the bottom again securely to form the first petal.

3 Continue making the petals by folding, turning and stitching until the rose in the desired size.

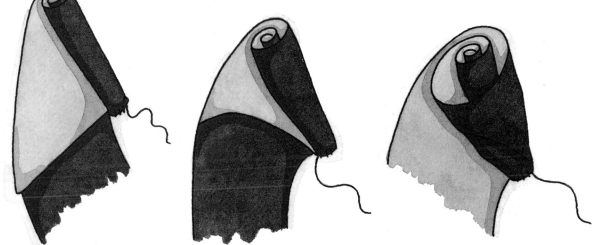

Rolling the centre and forming the first petal   *Forming the subsequent petals*

Rosebuds

Rosebuds are made more simply and stitched to a background with a few decorative stitches. Fold a 5cm (2in) square of ribbon in half diagonally, with the fold at the top. Bring the two outer corners to the lower corner folding one over the other. Gather the points together to form the bud. Stitch in place.

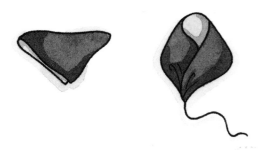

Folding a rosebud from a square of ribbon

Rosettes

These are easy to make in wire-edged ribbon. Simply draw up the ribbon along one edge of the wire, fasten the ends by twisting together with a pair of pliers. Turn in and stitch the raw edges of the ribbon to form the rosette. If you are using ordinary ribbon without wire, just gather along one edge, pull it tight and fasten off. Join the two ends together and stitch the rosette in place.

Gathering a rosette

*Facing page: **Evening bag with ribbon appliqué and roses***

OTHER TEXTILE TECHNIQUES

If you are experienced at textile techniques such as knitting, crochet, weaving, lacemaking or tatting, you can use your skills to create motifs or areas of design which can applied to a plain, painted or dyed surface. Even simple tubes of French knitting can be made into colourful edgings or stitched into different shapes as appliqué motifs.

Experiment with unconventional threads for all these techniques. There are many different yarns on the market which will give a variety of effects which can be used as backgrounds or elements in a design. You can even make threads for stitching, knitting or crochet from ribbons or torn narrow lengths of fine fabric such as muslin or silk.

Small fragments of knitting or crochet can be manipulated into different shapes by folding, pleating or ruching, adding texture to a piece or representing natural objects – little circlets of crochet make convincing flower shapes, and you can shape leaf forms by increasing and decreasing rows of knitting.

Exciting results can be achieved by altering the normal scale of a technique: using giant knitting needles for knitting with fine thread for a lacy effect, for example, or using chunky wool for needle lace stitches. Weaving and hand or machine knitting can be worked in a formal way with added colour applied using stencils, spray painting or dyes. Handmade lace or tatting can be partially dip-dyed or have areas of the pattern such as the centres of flower motifs transformed with paint. Macramé is an almost forgotten craft nowadays, but it remains one of the best techniques for making interesting braids and fringes for adding to soft furnishing items, clothes and accessories.

METALS AND FOILS

THE ADDITION OF non-traditional materials to fabrics is an exciting development in the textile world. It requires little skill and manufacturers have made life easy for the amateur by producing new products which are simple to use. Whether you are adding motifs in copper or brass, stitching metal wires to a background or working with metallic foils, the results will add an extra dimension and sparkle to your work.

Sheet metal and some foils are best used for items such as pictures, panels or wall hangings which are purely decorative, but most of the metallic foils are suitable for embellishing garments and accessories as well as soft furnishing items such as curtains and blinds. They have the added advantage that they can also be applied to other items for the home, including wallpaper, china and glassware so you can achieve a fully co-ordinated effect.

'IF YOU DESIRE WORDS' BY BEVERLEY J. FOLKARD. *Incorporating a photocopied poem, this mixed media piece uses woollen blanket, wrapping paper, plastic tubing, copper wire and gold metal ball chain*

METALS

Using metal sheet

Sheets of thin gauge brass, copper and aluminium are available from specialist suppliers and can be cut with strong kitchen scissors to the required shape to make small motifs. These can then be glued in place with a suitable adhesive or, if you prefer, holes can be pierced in the metal and the motif stitched to the background in the usual way with small stitches holding the metal in place. If you wish to make

a feature of the stitching you can use the methods described for attaching found objects (see page 110). Some of these products are so fine that they can be machine stitched, although the needle may blunt quickly and sometimes break. The most effective way to incorporate a motif so that it blends into the background is to work free-machining with straight or zigzag stitches (see page 75) to cover the edge. For

Embossed brass sheet is machine stitched with free zigzag in a variegated metal thread

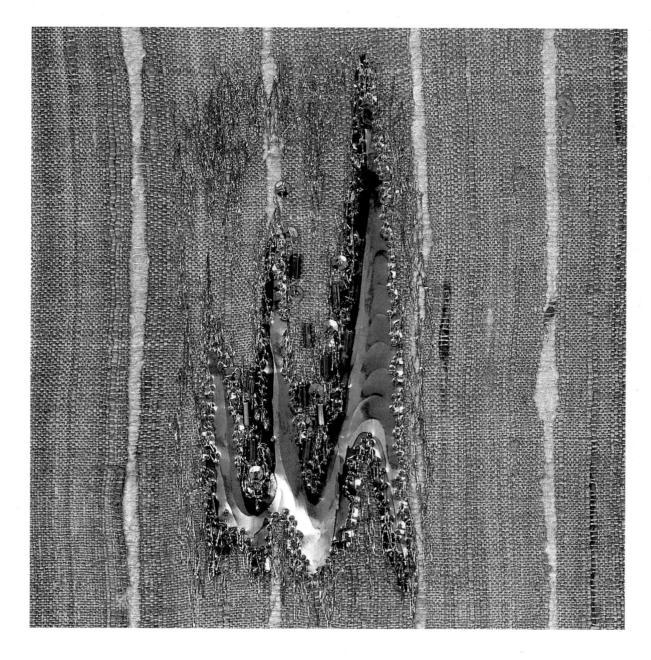

more formal designs you can use an open zigzag or straight stitching set to a long stitch.

If you wish to add areas of colour to the metal you can paint it with acrylic paint. For a more translucent effect, French enamels and paints used in model making are best. These thin gauge metals can also be embossed with patterns impressed on the reverse side. Place the metal sheet on a soft pad of newspapers, felt or wadding and draw lines or dots using a spent ballpoint pen or knitting needle.

Couching metal wires and strip

These thin wires and flat lengths of metal strip come in a variety of different gauges and colours. Copper strip with an adhesive backing is also an option and is useful for placing in straight lines or forming into geometric shapes. All these can be couched down in the usual way with unobtrusive or decorative stitches. If you prefer you can stitch by machine using a narrow zigzag or automatic stitch. A braiding foot can also be used.

Couching metal wire and strip

Metal meshes

These are available in copper, brass, aluminium and stainless steel in a range of gauges and sizes in either square or diamond-shaped form. Some of the range come in a selection of rich colours, but you can easily paint the mesh with enamel paint. The fine gauge can be cut easily into motifs for appliqué or manipulated into three-dimensional shapes and the wider meshes can be threaded with narrow ribbons, darned with a variety of different yarns or used as a mask for painting or spraying (see page 11). There is also a pliable micro-mesh which acts more like a stiff fabric which can be crumpled, ruched or pleated.

A sampler showing the use of metal mesh and strip, together with machine-couched copper wires

FOILS

One of the most exciting innovations in recent years has been the introduction of foils which give metallic effects to fabrics, papers, polymer clay, wood, etc. They come in a variety of guises but the most readily available are those which you press into a prepared surface and those which are applied using heat. Foils usually come in gold, silver and copper, as well as rich plain colours but some manufacturers produce striking metallic patterns, including hologram and mother-of-pearl effects.

Leaf metal foils

These foils work best on hard smooth surfaces such as wooden or polymer clay beads, but they can be applied to fabrics, particularly for items such as embroidered panels or pictures which will not be subjected to hard wear. The effects are very bright and can add a focal point or areas of special interest to a piece of work. The foiled surface will take on a similar texture to the fabric background, so a smooth fabric will give a more precise effect whilst on rough fabric the foil will break up into tiny fragments adding a textured look. You can work hand or machine stitches on top to soften the brightness or add beads for additional texture.

The paper-thin sheets of foil come in small booklets containing six 140 x 140mm (6 x 6in) sheets and you will also need a bottle of special size and some soft paint brushes and varnish or shellac. Make sure the surface to which you are applying the foil is clean and wrinkle-free.

1 Secure the fabric to the working surface with masking tape.

2 Apply a thin coat of size evenly across the surface and allow it to dry for about 20 minutes. Wash your brush in water.

3 Slide the foil from the booklet onto a piece of card and give a short sharp outward breath over it so it lies smoothly. It can then be cut with a sharp craft knife into manageable pieces.

4 Pick up a piece of foil with a wide-bladed knife and lay it on the sized surface. Don't worry if you have to overlap some of the pieces slightly. Press and smooth down with a soft brush or cloth and allow to dry for 24 hours.

5 If you are decorating wood or polymer clay, protect the foiled surface with a coat of varnish or shellac.

Using a foiling wand

These foils which are fully washable come in A4 sheets in a wide range of colours, including rainbow and hologram patterns. They are used in conjunction with an electrically operated wand which heats to exactly the right temperature to melt the colour so that it is transferred from the protective surface onto the fabric. A special foiling mat is also available which retains the heat and gives a good smooth pressing surface.

1 Lay the fabric on the foiling mat and plug in the foiling wand.

2 Place the section of foil colour side up on the fabric and push the foiling wand across the surface pressing firmly and evenly throughout.

3 Peel away the protective paper.

Foiling with rubber stamps

If you are not confident about drawing your own designs, rubber stamps (see page 35) offer a satisfactory alternative solution. Choose a stamp with a fine-lined design without too many solid areas.

1 Apply the bonding solution sparingly over the surface of the stamp using a sponge or brush.

2 Print in the usual way, pressing the stamp down vertically and evenly. Allow to dry for about three minutes.

3 Place the foil colour side up over the print and use a roller or the back of a spoon to adhere it to the surface. Peel away the foil.

Foiling with bonding web

Securing foil to fabric using bonding web (see page 90) is useful for solid areas of metallic effect including those with intricate outlines.

1 Draw the shape to be bonded on the paper side of the bonding web and cut out.

2 Position the cut-out shape rough side down onto the right side of the fabric and iron in place using as hot an iron as the fabric will allow. Peel away the backing paper.

3 Place the foil colour side up over the shape with a piece of greaseproof paper or baking parchment on top.

4 Reduce the temperature of the iron to 160°C wool setting and iron over the shape using heavy pressure for 3–5 seconds. Allow to cool and peel away the foil backing.

Vibrant multicoloured foils applied with adhesive and bonding web

Pressure-sensitive foiling

For raised metallic effects on velvets, wools and stretchy fabrics such as jerseys and knitwear, these foils are used with a special adhesive which comes in a plastic bottle with a nozzle.

1 Pre-wash the fabric if possible and lay it on a smooth, plastic covered work surface. Draw the design lightly with a disappearing fabric marker. This can be done free-hand or using a stencil (see page 17).

2 Apply the pressure-sensitive adhesive along the lines of the design and fill in any solid areas. Allow to dry for from four to 24 hours when it should be clear and solid, but still tacky.

3 Place the foil colour-side up and press gently with your fingers, using your fingernails or a blunt implement to push the foil into the edges. Peel away the foil from the surface.

Foiling pens

A development of pressure-sensitive foiling is a foiling pen whose adhesive dries in less than five minutes. This is particularly useful for writing and for intricate designs.

1 Tape the fabric to your work-surface using masking tape and draw the design directly with the foiling pen.

2 Allow to dry for a few minutes or speed up the process using a hairdryer held about 30cm (12in) away.

3 Place the foil colour-side up and rub gently with your fingers. Peel away the foil from the surface of the fabric.

Glitter effects

Glitter is available in a large number of exciting colours and it comes in two sizes. It is used in conjunction with pressure-sensitive adhesive (see above).

1 Work on a piece of paper which you have previously folded in half and opened out. This will make it easier to put excess glitter back into the container when you have finished.

2 Prepare the fabric and apply the adhesive as above.

3 Allow to dry until tacky.

4 Scoop a small amount of glitter on to an emery board and sprinkle it over the adhesive by tapping the emery board.

5 Shake off the excess glitter and allow to dry. If necessary, use a vacuum cleaner attachment to remove the excess glitter completely.

Special effects

Left-over scraps of foil can be used effectively if you apply them to the prepared surface through pieces of lace, wide mesh net or plastic fruit or vegetable nets. Build up layers of different colours until the tacky surface is completely covered with multicoloured foils.

GALLERY

◆

Featuring work by

ROZ ARNO

PAULINE BROWN

ANNA CHRISTY

ROSIE DANIELS

DIANA DOLMAN

NOEL DRYENFORTH

GRETA FITCHETT

MORAG GILBART

GLENYS GRIMWOOD

ELSPETH KEMP

ALISON KING

CHRIS LEWIS

YVONNE MORTON

MAGGIE PHILLIPS

TERESA SEARLE

ANN WHEELER

KAREN YOUNG

THIS GALLERY OF finished pieces by different textile artists shows the wide range of decoration which can be achieved using the techniques in this book. They show a wealth of effects using paint, dye and stitch as well as contemporary print media. Most are mixed media pieces whose inspiration has been sparked off in a variety of ways – by experimentation, drawing, or research. Studying these works will give you confidence to experiment and enable you to produce innovative and interesting results.

'TURKISH CARPET' GRETA FITCHETT 23 x 38IN (59 x 97CM). *Appliqué panel in a variety of different fabrics, embellished with free-machine embroidery*

'CHINCHINQUIRA' (DETAIL) GRETA FITCHETT. *Wall panel inspired by pre-Columbian South American artefacts, featuring recycled materials. Squares of felted and dyed wool blanket stitched with hand and machine embroidery*

'WHEN DARKNESS COVERED THE EARTH' ALISON
KING 48 X 48IN (122 X 122CM) (MAIN PANEL).
*A mixed media triptych which echoes medieval
and icon traditions and is concerned with the
element of surprise on opening the doors*

'ANEMONE MASK AND FAN' DIANA DOLMAN.
*Painted silk, machine embroidered
and hand stitched with beads
and semi-precious stone chips*

'SEED BOX' ANN WHEELER 13 X 9½IN (33 X 24CM).
*Three-dimensional piece with closing doors (not
shown) based on dried seed heads. Worked in
machine embroidery*

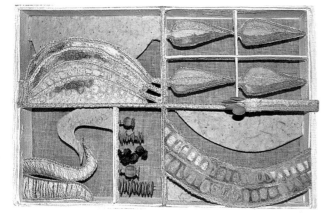

BATIK CUSHIONS ROZ ARNO.
Selection of silk cushions

'TRIBAL RHYTHMS' (DETAIL)
ANN WHEELER. *Part of a long
piece, based on African people
and patterns, which folds to be
contained in a box. Machine
and hand embroidery*

'WINTER TRAILS' CHRIS LEWIS 12 x 18IN
(45 x 30CM). *Handmade felt and paper, glass
nuggets and embroidery*

'BEACHCOMBING' CHRIS LEWIS 12 x 18IN
(45 x 30CM). *Hanging made of
handmade felt with a silk inlay,
embroidery with added driftwood, shells,
beach glass and old drinks cans*

'FULL OF EASTERN PROMISE' MORAG GILBART
17 x 24IN (43 x 61CM). *Raised wool with
hand and machine embroidery*

'FANTASY GARDEN' (DETAIL) DIANA DOLMAN. *Part of a panel, machine embroidered and hand stitched with beads*

'VOICE 1' KAREN YOUNG 7 X 11½IN (19 X 29CM). *Abstract piece inspired by a Thomas Hardy poem. Painted paper and dyed fabrics with hand and machine embroidery*

'PATHWAY TO HEAVEN' YVONNE MORTON 48 X 48IN (122 X 122CM). *Layers of cut-away organzas and metallic fabrics together with some appliqué on a base of dyed felt (photographed by Photoshades)*

'THE FOOL'S ACHIEVEMENT' YVONNE MORTON 24 X 26IN (61 X 66CM). *Based on heraldic research in appliqué, reverse appliqué together with gold leaf*

'AKETON' YVONNE MORTON 25 X 32IN (64 X 80CM). *Reverse appliqué technique, using layers of organza, metallic fabrics and some appliqué, with dyed felt as a base*

'MONEMVASIA COURTYARD' ANNA CHRISTY
14 x 10IN (35 x 26CM). *A Greek courtyard and
terrace. Watercolour on canvas with hand dyed
fabric and paper fragments together with
machine and hand stitches*

'CORTINHAS 1' ANNA CHRISTY 17 x 13IN
(44 x 33CM). *The Portuguese landscape with
its red earth, wild cistus flowers and
periwinkle inspired this piece with its layers
of silks, organza, muslin and silk paper*

'TEMPLE, PETRA' (DETAIL) ALISON KING.
*Inspired by a visit to Petra, Jordan, with
its temples cut into the stratified rock.
Machine embroidery on handmade
paper, felt, printed and marbled papers*

'SPRING LEVELS' KAREN YOUNG 6 x 9½IN
(15 x 24CM). *The Somerset levels inspired
this piece in machine appliqué in a variety
of fabrics with hand embroidery*

'SUMMER GARDEN' (DETAIL)
GRETA FITCHETT. *Appliquéd
nasturtiums, with hand and
machine embroidery*

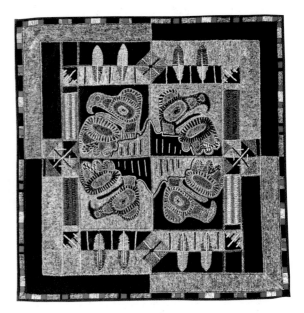

'THE LONGEST DAY' ELSPETH KEMP 30 x 48IN (76 x 122CM). *A multimedia work made to commemorate D-Day, using hand and machine appliqué and stitchery combined with fabric paints and oil paint sticks* (photographed by Barry Gould)

'THUNDERBIRD' ELSPETH KEMP 27 x 27IN (68 x 68CM). *North American Indian designs influenced the design for this hanging of inlaid felts with paint and stitchery* (photographed by Ad Shots Studio, Hertford)

'STONES AT THE FOREST EDGE' ALISON KING 48 x 48IN (122 x 122CM) (MAIN PANEL). *Inspired by the stones at Kenmore, a mixed media triptych with handmade papers, batik, tie-dye, and paint*

'FIREBIRD' NOEL DYRENFORTH
16 X 16IN (40 X 40CM). *Wax resist
with two types of dye on silk (Private
collection of Mr & Mrs Snook)*

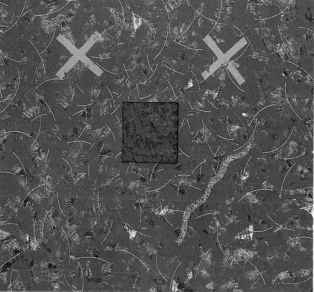

'ADRIFT' NOEL DYRENFORTH 57 X 64IN
(144 X 162CM). *Wax resist and discharge
dyeing on cotton, commissioned for the
reception area of HQ Global Workplaces,
Bishopsgate, London*

'AUTUMN GARDEN' MAGGIE PHILLIPS
9 x 9IN (23 x 23CM). *Canvas overlaid
with organza, and stitchery with
applied painted velvet.*

'CYCLAMEN' (DETAIL) MAGGIE
PHILLIPS. *A canvaswork piece
with spray dyeing and applied
cut and painted velvet*

'MANUSCRIPTS AND
MAGNOLIAS' MAGGIE
PHILLIPS 18 x 25IN
(46 x 64CM). *An idea
taken from the 'Book
of Kells' with painted
background, burden
stitch roundels and
applied flowers in
painted and cut velvet*

'TROPICAL SEASCAPE' PAULINE
BROWN 12 x 8IN (30 x 20 CM).
*A variety of organzas and silks
with frayed edges, held in place
with straight and zigzag
machine stitches*

'AND THE WORD BECAME
FLESH' GLENYS GRIMWOOD
33 x 33IN (85 x 85CM).
*An ecclesiastical hanging in
machine appliqué in silk for
the Coplestone Centre in
south-east London*

'TORAN' PAULINE BROWN 18 X 27IN (46 X 69CM). *Silk appliqué with frayed edges combined with tie-dyed fabric for a hanging inspired by Indian decorative friezes*

SILK TIES, ROSIE DANIELS. *A selection of silk-painted ties using a variety of different techniques*

BOOK, PAULINE BROWN. *Marbled fabric with woven wheels and couching in metallic threads*

BAG, ELSPETH KEMP 8 X 7IN (20 X 18CM). *Machine embroidery with metallic and cotton threads on organza mounted on red wool, some paint stick decoration added*

SMALL HANDBAGS, TERESA SEARLE. *Machine knitted felted wool with machine appliqué decoration in the same hand-made fabric (photographed by Nigel Currivan)*

INDEX

ILLUSTRATIONS

ABOUT THE AUTHOR

PAULINE BROWN is an expert quilter and teacher of embroidery, patchwork and textile crafts. She has already written a number of well-received books on embroidery and appliqué, including *The Creative Quilter* and *Patchwork for Beginners*, also published by GMC Publications (see next page).

OTHER GMC TITLES
BY PAULINE BROWN

Patchwork for Beginners

An introduction to this simple, satisfying and absorbing craft which covers the full range of techniques for perfecting patchwork designs.

Follow Pauline's ideas, using gorgeous colour combinations and easy patterns, to make some delightful gifts and decorative items for the home, including:

- evening bag • place mats • sewing set
- tissue-box cover • pin cushion
- cushions • Amish-style quilt • cot quilt
- wall hanging • cot quilt • throw
- Christmas decorations • toy cat

The Creative Quilter

This comprehensive guide to quilting offers practical advice for the beginner and great ideas for the experienced. An extensive chapter on techniques covers a wide range of quilting styles. The projects show how quilting can be used to create wonderful, colourful and useful items for the home.

All the basics are covered in detail, from the small range of inexpensive equipment required to the simple stitches used. Clear step-by-step colour illustrations lead you through each stage of the process, helping you create projects which include:

- silk and calico cushions • toy bag tidy
- Art Nouveau photo frame
- colourful play mat • heirloom cot quilt • evening bag and scarf

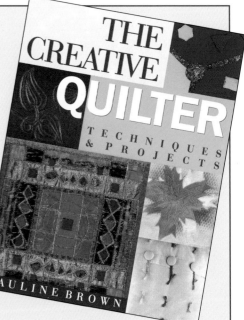

TITLES AVAILABLE FROM
GMC PUBLICATIONS

BOOKS

WOODCARVING

The Art of the Woodcarver — *GMC Publications*
Carving Architectural Detail in Wood:
The Classical Tradition — *Frederick Wilbur*
Carving Birds & Beasts — *GMC Publications*
Carving the Human Figure: Studies in Wood and Stone
— *Dick Onians*
Carving Nature: Wildlife Studies in Wood
— *Frank Fox-Wilson*
Carving Realistic Birds — *David Tippey*
Decorative Woodcarving — *Jeremy Williams*
Elements of Woodcarving — *Chris Pye*
Essential Woodcarving Techniques — *Dick Onians*
Further Useful Tips for Woodcarvers — *GMC Publications*
Lettercarving in Wood: A Practical Course — *Chris Pye*
Making & Using Working Drawings for Realistic Model
Animals — *Basil F. Fordham*
Power Tools for Woodcarving — *David Tippey*
Practical Tips for Turners & Carvers — *GMC Publications*
Relief Carving in Wood: A Practical Introduction *Chris Pye*
Understanding Woodcarving — *GMC Publications*
Understanding Woodcarving in the Round
— *GMC Publications*
Useful Techniques for Woodcarvers — *GMC Publications*
Wildfowl Carving – Volume 1 — *Jim Pearce*
Wildfowl Carving – Volume 2 — *Jim Pearce*
Woodcarving: A Complete Course — *Ron Butterfield*
Woodcarving: A Foundation Course — *Zoë Gertner*
Woodcarving for Beginners — *GMC Publications*
Woodcarving Tools & Equipment Test Reports
— *GMC Publications*
Woodcarving Tools, Materials & Equipment — *Chris Pye*

WOODTURNING

Adventures in Woodturning — *David Springett*
Bert Marsh: Woodturner — *Bert Marsh*
Bowl Turning Techniques Masterclass — *Tony Boase*
Colouring Techniques for Woodturners — *Jan Sanders*
Contemporary Turned Wood: New Perspectives in a Rich
Tradition — *Ray Leier, Jan Peters & Kevin Wallace*
The Craftsman Woodturner — *Peter Child*
Decorative Techniques for Woodturners — *Hilary Bowen*
Fun at the Lathe — *R.C. Bell*
Illustrated Woodturning Techniques — *John Hunnex*

Intermediate Woodturning Projects — *GMC Publications*
Keith Rowley's Woodturning Projects — *Keith Rowley*
Practical Tips for Turners & Carvers — *GMC Publications*
Turning Green Wood — *Michael O'Donnell*
Turning Miniatures in Wood — *John Sainsbury*
Turning Pens and Pencils — *Kip Christensen*
— *& Rex Burningham*
Understanding Woodturning — *Ann & Bob Phillips*
Useful Techniques for Woodturners — *GMC Publications*
Useful Woodturning Projects — *GMC Publications*
Woodturning: Bowls, Platters, Hollow Forms,
Vases, Vessels, Bottles, Flasks, Tankards, Plates
— *GMC Publications*
Woodturning: A Foundation Course
(New Edition) — *Keith Rowley*
Woodturning: A Fresh Approach — *Robert Chapman*
Woodturning: An Individual Approach — *Dave Regester*
Woodturning: A Source Book of Shapes — *John Hunnex*
Woodturning Jewellery — *Hilary Bowen*
Woodturning Masterclass — *Tony Boase*
Woodturning Techniques — *GMC Publications*
Woodturning Tools & Equipment Test Reports
— *GMC Publications*
Woodturning Wizardry — *David Springett*

WOODWORKING

Advanced Scrollsaw Projects — *GMC Publications*
Bird Boxes and Feeders for the Garden — *Dave Mackenzie*
Complete Woodfinishing — *Ian Hosker*
David Charlesworth's Furniture-Making Techniques
— *David Charlesworth*
The Encyclopedia of Joint Making — *Terrie Noll*
Furniture & Cabinetmaking Projects — *GMC Publications*
Furniture-Making Projects for the Wood Craftsman
— *GMC Publications*
Furniture-Making Techniques for the Wood Craftsman
— *GMC Publications*
Furniture Projects — *Rod Wales*
Furniture Restoration (Practical Crafts) — *Kevin Jan Bonner*
Furniture Restoration and Repair for Beginners
— *Kevin Jan Bonner*
Furniture Restoration Workshop — *Kevin Jan Bonner*
Green Woodwork — *Mike Abbott*
Kevin Ley's Furniture Projects — *Kevin Ley*

Making & Modifying Woodworking Tools   *Jim Kingshott*
Making Chairs and Tables   *GMC Publications*
Making Classic English Furniture   *Paul Richardson*
Making Little Boxes from Wood   *John Bennett*
Making Screw Threads in Wood   *Fred Holder*
Making Shaker Furniture   *Barry Jackson*
Making Woodwork Aids and Devices   *Robert Wearing*
Mastering the Router   *Ron Fox*
Minidrill: Fifteen Projects   *John Everett*
Pine Furniture Projects for the Home   *Dave Mackenzie*
Practical Scrollsaw Patterns   *John Everett*
Router Magic: Jigs, Fixtures and Tricks to
    Unleash your Router's Full Potential   *Bill Hylton*
Routing for Beginners   *Anthony Bailey*
The Scrollsaw: Twenty Projects   *John Everett*
Sharpening: The Complete Guide   *Jim Kingshott*
Sharpening Pocket Reference Book   *Jim Kingshott*
Simple Scrollsaw Projects   *GMC Publications*
Space-Saving Furniture Projects   *Dave Mackenzie*
Stickmaking: A Complete Course   *Andrew Jones*
    & Clive George
Stickmaking Handbook   *Andrew Jones & Clive George*
Test Reports: *The Router* and *Furniture & Cabinetmaking*
    GMC Publications
Veneering: A Complete Course   *Ian Hosker*
Veneering Handbook   *Ian Hosker*
Woodfinishing Handbook (Practical Crafts)   *Ian Hosker*
Woodworking with the Router: Professional
    Router Techniques any Woodworker can Use
    Bill Hylton & Fred Matlack
The Workshop   *Jim Kingshott*

UPHOLSTERY

The Upholsterer's Pocket Reference Book   *David James*
Upholstery: A Complete Course
(Revised Edition)   *David James*
Upholstery Restoration   *David James*
Upholstery Techniques & Projects   *David James*
Upholstery Tips and Hints   *David James*

TOYMAKING

Designing & Making Wooden Toys   *Terry Kelly*
Fun to Make Wooden Toys & Games   *Jeff & Jennie Loader*
Restoring Rocking Horses   *Clive Green & Anthony Dew*
Scrollsaw Toy Projects   *Ivor Carlyle*
Scrollsaw Toys for All Ages   *Ivor Carlyle*
Wooden Toy Projects   *GMC Publications*

DOLLS' HOUSES AND MINIATURES

1/12 Scale Character Figures for the Dolls' House
    James Carrington
Architecture for Dolls' Houses   *Joyce Percival*
The Authentic Georgian Dolls' House   *Brian Long*

A Beginners' Guide to the Dolls' House Hobby
    Jean Nisbett
Celtic, Medieval and Tudor Wall Hangings in 1/12 Scale
Needlepoint   *Sandra Whitehead*
The Complete Dolls' House Book   *Jean Nisbett*
The Dolls' House 1/24 Scale: A Complete Introduction
    Jean Nisbett
Dolls' House Accessories, Fixtures and Fittings
    Andrea Barham
Dolls' House Bathrooms: Lots of Little Loos   *Patricia King*
Dolls' House Fireplaces and Stoves   *Patricia King*
Dolls' House Window Treatments   *Eve Harwood*
Easy to Make Dolls' House Accessories   *Andrea Barham*
Heraldic Miniature Knights   *Peter Greenhill*
How to Make Your Dolls' House Special:
Fresh Ideas for Decorating   *Beryl Armstrong*
Make Your Own Dolls' House Furniture   *Maurice Harper*
Making Dolls' House Furniture   *Patricia King*
Making Georgian Dolls' Houses   *Derek Rowbottom*
Making Miniature Food and Market Stalls   *Angie Scarr*
Making Miniature Gardens   *Freida Gray*
Making Miniature Oriental Rugs & Carpets
    Meik & Ian McNaughton
Making Period Dolls' House Accessories   *Andrea Barham*
Making Tudor Dolls' Houses   *Derek Rowbottom*
Making Victorian Dolls' House Furniture   *Patricia King*
Miniature Bobbin Lace   *Roz Snowden*
Miniature Embroidery for the Georgian Dolls' House
    Pamela Warner
Miniature Embroidery for the Victorian Dolls' House
    Pamela Warner
Miniature Needlepoint Carpets   *Janet Granger*
More Miniature Oriental Rugs & Carpets
    Meik & Ian McNaughton
Needlepoint 1/12 Scale:
Design Collections for the Dolls' House   *Felicity Price*
The Secrets of the Dolls' House Makers   *Jean Nisbett*

CRAFTS

American Patchwork Designs in Needlepoint
    Melanie Tacon
A Beginners' Guide to Rubber Stamping   *Brenda Hunt*
Blackwork: A New Approach   *Brenda Day*
Celtic Cross Stitch Designs   *Carol Phillipson*
Celtic Knotwork Designs   *Sheila Sturrock*
Celtic Knotwork Handbook   *Sheila Sturrock*
Celtic Spirals and Other Designs   *Sheila Sturrock*
Collage from Seeds, Leaves and Flowers   *Joan Carver*
Complete Pyrography   *Stephen Poole*
Contemporary Smocking   *Dorothea Hall*
Creating Colour with Dylon   *Dylon International*
Creative Doughcraft   *Patricia Hughes*
Creative Embroidery Techniques Using Colour Through
Gold   *Daphne J. Ashby & Jackie Woolsey*

The Creative Quilter: Techniques and Projects
Pauline Brown
Decorative Beaded Purses *Enid Taylor*
Designing and Making Cards *Glennis Gilruth*
Glass Engraving Pattern Book *John Everett*
Glass Painting *Emma Sedman*
Handcrafted Rugs *Sandra Hardy*
How to Arrange Flowers: A Japanese
Approach to English Design *Taeko Marvelly*
How to Make First-Class Cards *Debbie Brown*
An Introduction to Crewel Embroidery *Mave Glenny*
Making and Using Working Drawings for Realistic Model
Animals *Basil F. Fordham*
Making Character Bears *Valerie Tyler*
Making Decorative Screens *Amanda Howes*
Making Fairies and Fantastical Creatures *Julie Sharp*
Making Greetings Cards for Beginners *Pat Sutherland*
Making Hand-Sewn Boxes: Techniques and Projects
Jackie Woolsey
Making Knitwear Fit *Pat Ashforth & Steve Plummer*
Making Mini Cards, Gift Tags & Invitations
Glennis Gilruth
Making Soft-Bodied Dough Characters *Patricia Hughes*
Natural Ideas for Christmas: Fantastic Decorations to
Make *Josie Cameron-Ashcroft & Carol Cox*
Needlepoint: A Foundation Course *Sandra Hardy*
New Ideas for Crochet: Stylish Projects for the Home
Darsha Capaldi
Patchwork for Beginners *Pauline Brown*
Pyrography Designs *Norma Gregory*
Pyrography Handbook (Practical Crafts) *Stephen Poole*
Ribbons and Roses *Lee Lockheed*
Rose Windows for Quilters *Angela Besley*
Rubber Stamping with Other Crafts *Lynne Garner*
Sponge Painting *Ann Rooney*
Stained Glass: Techniques and Projects *Mary Shanahan*
Step-by-Step Pyrography Projects for the Solid Point
Machine *Norma Gregory*
Tassel Making for Beginners *Enid Taylor*
Tatting Collage *Lindsay Rogers*
Temari: A Traditional Japanese Embroidery Technique
Margaret Ludlow
Theatre Models in Paper and Card *Robert Burgess*
Trip Around the World: 25 Patchwork, Quilting and
Appliqué Projects *Gail Lawther*
Trompe l'Oeil: Techniques and Projects *Jan Lee Johnson*
Wool Embroidery and Design *Lee Lockheed*

GARDENING

Auriculas for Everyone: How to Grow and Show Perfect
Plants *Mary Robinson*
Beginners' Guide to Herb Gardening *Yvonne Cuthbertson*
Bird Boxes and Feeders for the Garden *Dave Mackenzie*
The Birdwatcher's Garden *Hazel & Pamela Johnson*

Broad-Leaved Evergreens *Stephen G. Haw*
Companions to Clematis: Growing Clematis with Other
Plants *Marigold Badcock*
Creating Contrast with Dark Plants *Freya Martin*
Creating Small Habitats for Wildlife in your Garden
Josie Briggs
Gardening with Wild Plants *Julian Slatcher*
Growing Cacti and Other Succulents in the Conservatory
and Indoors *Shirley-Anne Bell*
Growing Cacti and Other Succulents in the Garden
Shirley Anne Bell
Hardy Perennials: A Beginner's Guide *Eric Sawford*
The Living Tropical Greenhouse: Creating a Haven for
Butterflies *John & Maureen Tampion*
Orchids are Easy: A Beginner's Guide to their Care and
Cultivation *Tom Gilland*
Plant Alert: A Garden Guide for Parents *Catherine Collins*
Planting Plans for Your Garden *Jenny Shukman*
Plants that Span the Seasons *Roger Wilson*
Sink and Container Gardening Using Dwarf Hardy Plants
Chris & Valerie Wheeler

PHOTOGRAPHY

An Essential Guide to Bird Photography *Steve Young*
Light in the Landscape: A Photographer's Year
Peter Watson

VIDEOS

Drop-in and Pinstuffed Seats *David James*
Stuffover Upholstery *David James*
Elliptical Turning *David Springett*
Woodturning Wizardry *David Springett*
Turning Between Centres: The Basics *Dennis White*
Turning Bowls *Dennis White*
Boxes, Goblets and Screw Threads *Dennis White*
Novelties and Projects *Dennis White*
Classic Profiles *Dennis White*
Twists and Advanced Turning *Dennis White*
Sharpening the Professional Way *Jim Kingshott*
Sharpening Turning & Carving Tools *Jim Kingshott*
Bowl Turning *John Jordan*
Hollow Turning *John Jordan*
Woodturning: A Foundation Course *Keith Rowley*
Carving a Figure: The Female Form *Ray Gonzalez*
The Router: A Beginner's Guide *Alan Goodsell*
The Scroll Saw: A Beginner's Guide *John Burke*

MAGAZINES

THE DOLLS' HOUSE MAGAZINE
WATER GARDENING
OUTDOOR PHOTOGRAPHY
BLACK & WHITE PHOTOGRAPHY
WOODTURNING ◆
WOODCARVING
FURNITURE & CABINETMAKING
THE ROUTER ◆ WOODWORKING
BUSINESSMATTERS

The above represents a full list of all titles currently published or scheduled to be published.
All are available direct from the Publishers or through bookshops, newsagents and specialist retailers.
To place an order, or to obtain a complete catalogue, contact:

GMC Publications,
Castle Place, 166 High Street,
Lewes, East Sussex BN7 1XU,
United Kingdom
Tel: 01273 488005 Fax: 01273 478606
E-mail: pubs@thegmcgroup.com

Orders by credit card are acccpted